Hello Friend

A Journey in ECK

Hello Friend
A Journey in ECK

Patti Simpson

Illuminated Way
Publishing Inc.
PO Box 28130
Crystal, MN 55428

HELLO FRIEND
A Journey in ECK

Printed in U.S.A.

ISBN: 0-88155-031-0

Library of Congress Catalog Card Number: 81-80176

Revised Edition—1984
Fourth Printing—1987

Cover Design and Illustration by
Phil Morimitsu

lovingly dedicated

to you, the seeker

and

to pete

Acknowledgement

For valuable assistance on this book in the outer world special thanks are due to: Monte Miller, Connie Murphy, Joy Laho, Daye Alvarez, Archeleen Hurst, Richard Orshoff, Barbara Dubin, Phil Wellman and Roger Dubin.

Table of Contents

1 The Theatre of Soul 7

2 How Will You Play Your Part? 33

3 Contemplation: Opening Night 51

4 The Plot Thickens: Paradox
  Island 75

5 The Program vs. Programming 91

6 The Bad Guys and The
  Good Guys 109

7 The Music: The Beat of Your
  Own Drum 123

8 Program Notes 135

9 The Leading Man 159

10 Why a Director 187

11 The Magic of It All 197

12 The Creative Backer: Author of
   Everything 205

Away O soul! hoist instantly the anchor!
Cut the hawsers—haul out—shake out every sail!
Have we not stood here like trees in the ground long enough?

—Walt Whitman
Leaves of Grass

1 The Theatre of Soul

Introduction

It was one o'clock in the morning, in the Spring of 1980, when I was awakened by you. At first I thought it was time to get up. I turned and looked at the clock, groaned, rolled over pulling the covers over my head and tried to do what I've learned is hopeless: go back to sleep.

One o'clock in the morning is the magic hour here. The creative force finds its way to me when the rest of the city sleeps, and since I'm not one to remember many of my dreams, it feels obliged to wake me up. I always groan, always try in vain to go back to sleep, always end up with some work to do... and I'm usually glad it happened.

In this case, I was very happy and excited because the book you are holding was spread out before me. And you were there. Perhaps you will not even become a student of Eckankar until long after this book appears in print, but at its writing you were there. I felt your presence, heard your questions, and knew what you were going through. That was possible because where these things happen, time and space do not exist.

I know a lot about you. You have carried long within you a deep yearning to know more about the nature of things. In your quiet moments you have asked yourself strange questions. *Who am I? Where did I come from? Why am I here? Where am I going?* You wondered about these things even as a small child. And while the questions are common among humans, you are not, because you stubbornly believe answers to these questions are possible.

You have within you the seeds of a revolutionary; a pioneer. You sense or know there is far more to existence than is commonly accepted and you can't help being curious about the unknown, although there are moments when you wish it weren't thus; moments when you wish you could be as satisfied and accepting of the safe, traditional forms as others seem to be. At one time or another you have tried to believe as others do, to conform to ideas and systems that are an established part of society. But always it would come, the forbidden question, the sense that this or that belief had you trapped inside a box.

At some point in all this you have

experienced anger. You felt angry because you were made to feel guilty for questioning, because you saw that the religions, the sciences, the educational and political systems all have their built-in controls, their red-lines, beyond which one cannot construct a reality without facing ostracism, threats, or ridicule. This annoys you because you are aware that many things which were said to be impossible, to be aberrations of a lunatic fringe, as recently as twenty years ago, are now being seriously studied and documented in the research departments of major universities.

You have within you a built-in aversion to certain words and phrases, to certain concepts. Among them are: Control. Limits. "You Can't." Right/Wrong. Impossible. "It's only your imagination." Sin. Hell. Damnation. "To question is to be lacking in faith." "There are two ways to do a thing: our way and the wrong way."

Such concepts as these tend to send you up the wall. Whether or not you have it concretely defined in your mind, something about it makes you uncomfortable, a bit angry, and hungry for space to grow in.

You didn't tell me all this specifically when we met in the middle of the night. What you conveyed to me was that we are very much alike, you and I. And so, I have just written for you a fairly accurate description of me as I approached the path of Eckankar. There's a name for this condition that we have. It's called "Divine Discontent." It is the mark of the Seeker. And when I meet one, I call him or her, Friend.

I am not altogether comfortable about writing a book using the first person singular. But in considering what there was to say, and to whom, it seemed forgiveable, even a necessity for three reasons. First, it began as an experience between us. You have a right to know who this person is who is sharing these things with you. As a student, a teacher, writer and lecturer of Eckankar for many years, I am acquainted with the joys and victories, the questions, side trips and the fears of this journey. In my functions as teacher and writer, I've worked personally, and through correspondence, with thousands of chelas. The one thing I won't say is that I've seen it all. But a lot. Certainly enough to cover a good part of the territory surrounding the new person taking up these studies. In addition to my regular studies, I have had the privilege and honor to work on a personal basis with three extraordinary spiritual beings: Sri Paul Twitchell, the founder of the present day Eckankar movement, Darwin Gross, his successor, and Sri Harold Klemp, the current Mahanta, Living ECK Master. Harold, who is known in the spiritual worlds as Wah Z, accepted the ECK Rod of Power on October 22, 1981. Although it is at the expense of my privacy at times, and my dignity at others, through this dialogue I am beginning to see that one of the reasons I was allowed to be so close to the private lives and inner workings of these Masters was because I had the tools and abilities to share the experience with others.

The second reason for writing in the first person was because I would be sharing many personal experiences. Not because mine are so wonderful but because they are mine. They are the basis for any expertise I may have. I will be emphasizing this again and again as we go along. We can read every book and discourse written on the ECK teachings. We can memorize them verbatim. We can hear the Living ECK Master speak a hundred times and ask a million questions of our teachers and spiritual leaders, but all of this will be for nothing if we do not experience it in our daily lives. Therefore, we cannot simply be information gatherers. ECK is not an intellectual exercise. It is your own personal tool kit. And a tool kit is not something to think about, to look at, to talk about, to take up space in your universe. A tool kit is nothing unless you are using it, fixing things with it, building wonderful creations that matter to you.

Eckankar is also called "The Ancient Science of Soul Travel." At other times it has been called "The Path of Total Awareness" and "A Way of Life." All of these definitions are true.

However, it is an ancient science, an applied science. You can achieve total awareness, but it won't do you much good if you're only going to sit on a mountaintop and contemplate your navel. It *is* a way of life, and for it to work for you it's necessary to filter what you learn through your experience of life.

At first you won't know how, you may be a bit confused and uncertain. Not to worry. It will become easier as you go along. Easier yet if you can be relaxed and confident, and that's the real purpose of my writing to you.

The third reason this is written in the tiresome "I" is the most important. Although it will come to you in the physical form of a book, this is a series of personal letters from me to you. No matter what ground we cover, that is the link I preserve and keep constantly in my consciousness.

The journey of Soul is, in reality, a journey through and out of the worlds of illusion. This illusion is a drama produced and directed by the Creator for the experience and edification of Soul. Perhaps the real meaning of "God-Realization" is total awareness regarding the play-quality of the world we live in and of our lives here. In that matter, then, success lies in the shift from an actor with an assigned rôle to director to producer to writer to First Cause.

The experience of Eckankar is really a play within the play. How does it work? How can we use it to make our way back to being First Cause? Come—walk awhile with me. If I've heard you rightly, there may be something for you in the pages ahead.

The Play Begins

The first initiation is a difficult thing to understand mainly because it is not a "planned event" as are subsequent initiations. Some say that it occurs when one first signs up for monthly discourses. This is not always the case. There are some people, spiritual shoppers, who sign up for everything. In the real estate business they're called "The Looky Loos." I seriously doubt that a non-seeker who is just looking or those who might have ulterior motives experience any kind of initiation.

On the other hand, there are Looky Loos who tell themselves that's what they are doing, only to discover later that Soul was very much in control of the operation and merely allowed the little white lie so the human vehicle would be comfortable and cooperate. It's happened to me so often I even have a name for it: The B.S. Factor. These individuals are definitely first initiates. I was one of them. For me it was a defiant, rebellious, hilarious game. I played at it for a year.

One night, a small meeting was scheduled in Los Angeles for students only. Paul Twitchell wanted to talk to them. I went out of curiosity—to see a famous author and to see what these people called ECKists looked like. Although I'd been reading the discourses for over half a year, I certainly didn't think I was one of *them*. I wouldn't have been surprised to see they had green hair and pointed ears.

I kept looking around the room trying to spot an ECKist. But all I saw were ordinary people, just like me. It was quite unsettling. Then Paul Twitchell came in and walked to the lectern. My thoughts about him that night, my impressions, are as vivid today as they were when they occurred. I would like to say I was disappointed, but I got just what I wanted—mostly. I wanted to be turned-off. I wanted to find fault. The one thing I did not want was to be impressed by him; to have to make some kind of commitment.

The first thing I noticed was that he was not very tall; kind of short, actually. He was wearing a rumpled blue suit, a blue shirt, and a blue, knitted, skinny tie, the kind that had already gone out of fashion. He was badly in need of a haircut as far as

I was concerned.

He started talking to the group and I noticed a strange combination of southern accent with British twists. He pronounced the word "again" as "agayne." At that particular time I had a strong prejudice against men with southern accents because I was mad as hell at Lyndon Johnson.

The next button of mine that he pushed was his grammar. I was raised to speak perfect English. Every time I slipped, my mother immediately corrected me. In time I got quite good at it and incorrect English would slap at my ears like a sour note in a musical recital. Needless to say, that night Paul Twitchell seemed to go out of his way to fracture the King's English. I say seemed to go out of his way, because I would hear him speak hundreds of times in the years to come. Later I would work at his side, listening to him for hours on end, and never again did I hear him do to the English language what he did that night. I have often wondered if he perpetrated that particular outrage solely for my benefit. To the uninitiated that statement may seem a tad conceited; however, in fact, the Masters often are prompted to initiate certain actions, often involving many others, sometimes the whole movement, for the particular learning experience of one single individual.

So, you get the picture: I'm sitting there with my opinions and my prejudices hanging out all over me. I did not come there to be impressed and certainly wasn't. At one point, as he looked around the room, he said, "You people have a lot of excess baggage to throw overboard." Just as he said this he sent out a look, long and piercing, in my direction. In that moment it seemed as if his gaze was a solid thing, a harpoon that went straight through me and nailed my body to the back of my chair. For an instant, it occurred to me that he actually meant *me*; that he might know what I was sitting there thinking. I experienced a moment of extreme discomfort, but managed to pass it off and continue to be unimpressed, as planned, for the remainder of his talk.

He finished and dismissed us and with a sigh of relief I stood to leave. "So that's that," I was telling myself, "and that's the last one of these things I'm coming to."

The crowd was moving very slowly toward the exit. Stuck in behind them, I turned and looked back at the stage. Paul Twitchell moved off the dais to a group of little, old ladies. One after another, in a tight circle, he embraced them. Something strange was happening. I stopped moving toward the door and stood there staring in fascination. They seemed to be surrounded, all of them, in an aura or circle of love that was so powerful I could see it with the naked eye. In spite of my resistance it was one of the most moving and compelling things I've ever seen. For a moment I stood there watching, feeling a strange yearning, and knowing I was very much on the outside. Then, suddenly, I shook myself loose from what I was seeing and hurried out the door. I practically ran from the place.

In the months that followed, and although I tried, there were two things I couldn't dismiss from my mind: One was that beautiful, almost palpable, circle of love I'd seen, and the other was the piercing gaze and the words, "You have a lot of excess baggage to throw overboard." Intellectually I didn't understand what that meant but in my subterranean caverns I knew. I knew he meant me, too.

The above story is not a common one.

But neither is it uncommon. Some people who come upon these teachings and take up the path are eager, cooperative co-workers with their Soul-self. Some, like me, have to be pushed, dragged along, and outmaneuvered by Soul. In the long run it really doesn't make much difference. Whatever direction it is that we must take, Soul will lead us by one means or another. By the time we're looking over this step, Soul is very much in control, even if we, as the human vehicle, are not yet even certain that such a thing as Soul exists.

Over the years I have participated in many workshops where ECKists relate the chain of events that preceded their decision to study Eckankar. I've heard these stories in private conversations, and have been sent many letters. I've also pored over letters in Paul's files. I have yet to hear a boring or mundane story.

In the early days there were very few public functions such as Introductory Lectures, Days of ECK, etc. The two main contacts, other than personal, were ads Paul placed in *Fate Magazine* and the books.

George was going to catch a bus in

Laguna Beach. Someone had left a book on the bus bench. He picked it up, riffled it, and slowly headed for the beach, the bus and his previous plan forgotten. He spent the entire day on the beach reading that book. It dramatically changed his life.

A shipyard worker in Long Beach was placing parts on warehouse shelves. He climbed a ladder and on the very top shelf, completely out of sight, he found a book. He took the book home and read it. Later, as a new student, he made his way to my house. He was thrilled that he had found, at last, what he'd been looking for since he was a child. But he was a troubled man. He felt terribly guilty because he had stolen someone's book. I began to laugh. I'd heard this story many times. Putting his guilt to rest, I said, "John, you did not steal anything. You cannot steal what is yours." Then I quoted to him from the book he thought he'd stolen, "When the chela is ready, the Master will find him." I knew about that one from first hand experience.

Not all of us start with books. Russell was sitting in his mobile home in Arizona drinking a cup of coffee when a knock came on the door. He opened the door to see a man in a blue suit standing there. He said the man was smiling and his face was very kind and gentle. He let him in. The man began to speak to him about matters he couldn't have known. He said, "I know you are divorced from your wife, Mary. But this was a mistake. The two of you have not finished what you had come together to do. If you would try again, both of you will benefit."

This information astonished Russell. He and Mary had been divorced for three years. Oddly, as the man in blue spoke, he realized how lonely he had been and that he would really like to be back with Mary, but he was pretty sure she'd have no part of it. He expressed this doubt. The man in blue smiled, "She will take you back," he said. And he was gone. Russell could not recall later hearing the door close. He also wondered later why he let the man talk to him about so intimate a subject without asking him who he was and how he came to know such things. What he did do was take a leave of absence from his job and head for California to see Mary.

When he arrived on her doorstep, Mary was surprised to see him. She invited him in and they sat for awhile and chatted uneasily. Russell awkwardly told her about his loneliness and his hope that she might consider trying it again. Mary was pretty turned off by the idea. The marriage hadn't gone well in the first place, and since she'd been on her own she'd made a lot of important personal changes she didn't feel like discussing with him.

He saw that his idea was not getting a good reception, and so he could think of nothing else to do but leave. As he walked past the dining room table he saw Mary's purse lying open, its contents strewn about as if, prior to his arrival, she'd dumped it out searching for something. Her billfold was lying open revealing the picture of a man. Russell jerked his head up in surprise. "Who is this man?" he asked. "Why do you want to know?" she replied defensively.

So Russell, who hadn't mentioned it before because it sounded so absurd, told her the story of the man in blue who'd come to his trailer and had urged the reunion. "That was the man, Mary, that is a picture of the man who talked to me. Who is he?" Mary was quiet and thoughtful for a long time. Finally she said, "The man in the picture is Paul Twitchell. He's my spiritual guide."

Mary and Russell sat in my living room and related this story. They were going to be remarried the next day. This is not a fairy tale. They were not wildly excited and magically in love once again. They were not at all certain that it was going to work out the second time around either. What they did feel was that they had left each other with *karma*, with unfinished business in the spiritual sense, and they needed to find out what that was and try again. Over the years, I lost track of them, so I can't tell you how it turned out, but if they read this, perhaps they'll get in touch and let us know. Incidentally, at the time Russell was being visited in Arizona by the man in blue, Paul Twitchell's physical body was at his home in San Diego, California.

Walt was having some strange inner experiences he couldn't explain, nor could any of the books he'd read explain them. There were times when he felt like something inside of him was trying to get out. He didn't know what it was, but it felt like his life force or his soul or something. He'd also been having vivid dreams in which he found himself in beautiful castles or temples and he was being tutored in ideas that were new and strange to him.

He found these experiences both fascinating and frightening. He was, at the time, working on his Ph.D. at a large midwestern university.

One day during a visit to his mother he began to speak tentatively of some of the things that were going on with him. His mother walked to her bookcase and pulled out a book by Paul Twitchell which she handed to him. "Maybe there's something in here you can use," she said.

Later, as he read the book, Walt became more and more excited. This was the exact information he'd been searching for. I heard Walt tell this story one night at an afterhour's rap at a seminar. We all laughed, it was a common enough story, but Walt's had its own individual twist. It seems that his mother had bought the book over a year before she gave it to him. For whatever reason, she had put it away. She had never read it. She didn't even know why she'd bought it. At the time Walt told us this story, he'd been an enthusiastic ECKist for three years. His mother still had never read an ECK book and showed absolutely no interest in doing so.

It is not an exaggeration to say that I could fill at least two fat books with the kind of stories I've just shared with you. Many people tell stories of experiences with Spiritual Travelers that go way back to their childhoods, of being saved from sure death, of someone appearing to them in the midst of serious illness or physical disability.

A friend of mine was crushed under a car when she was thirteen. She had broken bones all over her body. Her pelvis was crushed. The doctors said she'd never walk again. Certainly she'd never be able to bear children. But she was, and is, a strong and courageous Soul and "no" was a word that didn't fit in with her world. Slowly she came back. She did learn to walk again. But the one thing she had wanted since she was a very small child escaped her: She had always dreamed of becoming a dancer. She could walk, but her dreams of dancing had been crushed under that car. She carried the longing and the painful disappointment with her, well into her twenties. Fourteen years after her near fatal accident a mysterious being appeared to her. He gave her a command: "You may dance!" My friend is a gifted poet and she has told of this experience in poetry far better than I could write of it. She graciously gave permission to share it with you. Beyond its purely personal relationship to her experience, it has symbolic overtones that are also personal to many of us.

THE BALLET MASTER

Dreary room; it's like all others.
Wooden floor, worn from many feet,
Practice barres stretched over mirrors.
My eyes seek the door, to retreat...
Too late; his presence fills the room.
I had not seen him standing there
In the shadows; in my dim gloom
I lower my face from his stare.

Impressing dignity, he hovers
Magnetic; my attention's drawn
As an outstretched hand raises, lowers,
Giving me a silent command.

Has he heard? My very feelings
And thoughts stripped bare, by
   some odd chance!
The thought projects, clearly; reeling
My mind then perceives, "you may dance."
But I? I shriek mentally... how?
I've been told... I thought... I can not.
He speaks not, yet the word is, "now!"
And I dare think, it's not my lot!

For a split second then in time,
For just that moment, I believe
I can attain... it will be mine...
As cautiously I sway, and weave.

Again the piercing, gentle eyes
Command; I feel the love, and try
A tiny leap; I lift and rise,
I float on air, dreamlike, high!
I gasp with joy! "Again," I'm told
And suddenly I understand.
Overwhelming flows my courage, bold;
Gracefully, again I leap and land.

I've soared above reality
Unbounded by weight of earth and sea
Or captured Soul... and I am free!
This is the gift he's given me.

My friend did go on to dance, mastering the difficult and precise movements of the dances of the Indonesians and Balinese. She also, incidently, gave birth naturally to her children.

She never knew who the mysterious stranger was who had come to her in that shining experience until many years later when she became a student of Eckankar and the man appeared to her again in the identical way. This time his face was bathed in light and she recognized him. It was the Living ECK Master. As I said in the beginning, things like this are possible, because the dimension in which they occur does not deal with time and space.

These are some of the stories I've heard first hand. They are not more dramatic and special than all the others. If you trace your own journey back, you will find the signposts. The strange "coincidence" will no doubt pop up somewhere. You will find the magic moments when you retrace your footsteps. What was going through you at the moment you decided to call that number? Go to that particular place? Buy that book? Talk to that particular person? When you decided to write that first letter to Eckankar what were you thinking? All along your journey, when you go back over it, you will discover major and minor crossroads; a course of action you took, a choice you made that had another option, one that would have made things come out very differently. When you go back over your crossroads, it's a magical journey, for each choice, willing or forced, is the physical peephole through which you can observe the Soul-self making the calls. And if you haven't already discovered it, the word, "coincidence" will become a joke for you.

If you follow my suggestion, do this

review, somewhere in there you will find the moment, the special happening that was your first initiation. Maybe you knew without a shadow of doubt, or maybe you missed it because it wasn't flashy or mystical enough for your taste. Some people seem to think that if a thunderbolt came crashing out of the sky and lodged itself between their ears that would constitute a first initiation. They haven't considered that it could be as subtle as an unremembered dream from which they awakened feeling something different and unusual was about to take place. It could come from a stranger who suddenly smiles and looks into your eyes with a brief glance of recognition. Or it could be something like mine which happened in the dove pavilion of a Japanese park nearly a year before I collided with Paul Twitchell.

A dove flew up and landed on my hand and stood there fearlessly, pinning me with one copper eye. Although it was absurd, he seemed to know me, and there was the distinct sensation as he kept staring at me, that I knew him too. It was almost as if he was trying to say something to me through that intense, beady eye. For one instant, I thought he was going to give me some kind of message. I said, "Who are you?" But it was all too crazy. I looked at what was taking place and became so shook up that I dropped him and ran. I did a lot of running in those days. In spite of what I told myself, I was running *to* a very special appointment. Every choice I made from that day on led me inexorably to the teachings of Paul Twitchell.

I do not know whether I was then a man dreaming I was a butterfly, or whether I am now a butterfly dreaming I am a man.

—Chuang Tzu
369-286 B.C.

2 How Will You Play Your Part?

There are as many ways to do the spiritual path of Eckankar as there are individuals who are doing it. There are no demographics which can spell out who is likely to become an ECKist. We come from everywhere. There are students behind the Iron Curtain, nuns in convents, classes being held in countries where it is not only difficult, but dangerous. We come from every kind of religious and areligious background. We represent every social, economic, and educational strata; every race and age. At the yearly Eckankar World Wide Seminar you will see and hear and meet a total cross section of the planet.

At the World Wide of ECK seminar held in Baltimore in 1979, there were so many guests from overseas that translators were provided and much of the program was simultaneously translated into French as it took place.

One of the greatest gifts I have received from being active in Eckankar is the incredibly interesting people I have met from all over the world. Because of this, the world has become a very small place for me. To give you an idea of an ECK seminar, let me write a brief description of how it was in Baltimore in October 1979.

The seminar took place in the huge civic convention center. There were easily 5,000 people in the house. Off to one side sat a delegation of Africans from the Ivory Coast. During the parts of the program in which Darwin was not speaking, a chela from Italy sat among them and translated what was being said into French. Scattered about and mixing in with all the new friends they were making was a colorful group of ECKists from England, those of the Indian Sikh heritage. They are always a feast for the eyes; the men in beards and turbans, and the ladies in their colorful saris. These Indians have a thriving ECK community outside of London and produce an ECK newsletter that is written half in English and half in Punjabi.

Many have traveled to this seminar from Canada, and there is a good representation from Germany, Norway and Switzerland. The English, of course, are all over the place, and that beautiful, dark-eyed lady with her husband flew in from Panama. There's a lot of exclamations and hugging going on, for we have special bonds, many of long standing, and we don't see one another often enough although ECKists are the travelingest people I've ever met. I'm speaking here of the physical world, too.

The program is sprinkled with music and song. The young lady playing the hauntingly beautiful flute music is with the Brazil Symphony Orchestra to which she came from the Salzburg-Mozarteum Orchestra in Austria. Many of the musicians who will be playing here are professionals. All of them are ECKists.

Also on the program are a variety of speakers from all over the world. Some are the Higher Initiates of ECK, those unique individuals who are the Living ECK Master's personal representatives working out in the world. It is these Higher Initiates who carry the responsibilities equivalent to priests, bishops, ministers, etc., in other forms, although that is a simplification. They are the members of an elite spiritual brotherhood and much of the work each of them does for the Master is never seen or spoken of in public.

They are very special, these Brothers of

mine, but they are also humble. They are here to assist any student in trouble, and are always willing and happy to talk with those who seek them out. Mostly, you will not know who they are, unless someone points them out, or you've seen them on the stage giving a talk. If you want to speak with one, don't be shy. March right up and introduce yourself. It happens all the time, that's what we're there for. Incidentally, this group is not at all stuffy or swollen up with self-importance. They are notorious for their sense of humor and their ability to laugh at themselves. I'll tell you more about these folks later. For now let's just leave it at this: They are real people.

It's the evening program now. Those who've come to Baltimore for this event are scattered around the town in at least five hotels. During the day they come in and out of the auditorium, sometimes taking a break from the program to have a chat outside with anyone they happen to meet, or to browse through the book room. But in the evening, *everyone* is in the auditorium. There's a huge, expectant, restless kind of excitement. Small conversations take place, but everyone's inner attention is on that single stool, sitting out there in the center of the stage. No matter what we've seen and heard, the neat people we've met, the unusual experiences we've had, *this* is what we came here for: to see and hear the Living ECK Master.

The translator comes out and takes her place off to one side, and then the Living ECK Master of the time walks onto the stage. For the next half hour or so you can hear a pin drop in the huge auditorium. There are five thousand Souls each having their own private experience with what is being said here, what is being perceived. For those who are seeing the Master for the first time, it can be a very emotional experience.

I'm reminded of another seminar, many years ago. I was sitting next to a young lady who was new to the path. When the Master walked on the stage and began to speak, she began to come unglued. She was fidgeting and squirming and she appeared to be on the brink of tears. Finally I turned to her and whispered, "Is anything wrong?" "Oh," she said, "I'm *trying* to listen, but I can't make any sense of it. All I want to do is just sit and stare at him."

I giggled. She was doing a lot better than I did the first time I saw Paul. I didn't have the experience she was having until the second time I saw him. By then, I knew who he was, and more particularly, knew who he was to me. I had had the inner experience of him. That second time I didn't hear a word he said. My mind just refused to cope with it. The first time I'd let my mind stop him. The second time I just let the words sail over the top of the mind and make their way home to the inner self. For the rest, it was simply a joyous feast for my eyes. I understood the girl. I was delighted for her.

I stilled my giggles and spoke with all the knowing of a hotshot Higher Initiate.

"Don't worry about it. Soul will hear the words. You just sit there and enjoy yourself. Look to your heart's content. Drink it all in. That's just as much what he's here for as the words he's speaking."

Funny about that. I ran into that same girl in the book room here in Baltimore. She's a very calm, capable Initiate who is taking on a lot of responsibility in her area. Until she told the story to some people who were standing there with us, I hadn't associated this capable, dynamic woman with the perturbed, young girl I'd talked to way back there.

After hours at an ECK seminar are just as much a part of it all as the program. ECKists, in general, hate to go to bed at a seminar. In the hotel lobbies and coffee shops they gather in groups. There is always something nifty to hear, and lifelong friendships are made in chance encounters. Certainly ideas are proposed which seem uncannily to smack us right where we live. A casual comment can solve a huge question we'd been secretly chewing over for months.

Often folks meet and swear they've met before, only to be unable to pin it down after fruitless questioning. I don't know an ECKist who has not had this experience, and usually more than once. After awhile consternation turns to laughter. What can you finally think except that we've all made this trip more than once? And we're making it in more than one plane right now.

I've run the experience of a major seminar by you because I hoped to give you the sights, sounds, texture, feel, and possibilities of the experience. Maybe the experience is just not for you, either because it's physically not possible, as for those of you behind the Iron Curtain, or perhaps, it's not economically or geographically possible. Even so, when a major seminar is taking place, you can be there in spirit, and many are. I once heard a Higher Initiate say the crowd was much larger than it seemed, if you counted the ones there without skin on. Everybody laughed, but he was stating a fact. I have heard people insist that they saw this or that person at a particular seminar, even indignantly telling them exactly *where* they saw them and with *whom*. It does no good to tell them that you are quite sure you were *not* there. They *saw* you (in some cases they even *spoke* to you) and that's all there is to it. And, after all, are you *positive* you weren't there? . . . At least without your skin on?

But there are ECKists, some very special individuals, who quite simply have no need or desire to do their journey in a group or organizational context. For these ECKists, the path of Eckankar is an extremely personal journey, existing in a rich, highly active inner life. They study alone, they have a solid, viable relationship with the Inner Master, and their spiritual progress is daily manifested in their lives. It is possible to do this, and do it quite well, if that is your preference.

Some students who have blossomed and grown more than their fondest dreams by studying, interacting, and testing themselves in the outer organization have trouble understanding how anyone can do it alone. What they fail to recognize is that they are assuming that everyone is like them. And they make a larger mistake in assuming the people are doing it alone. No ECKist is ever alone. The Master is always there, as close to the chela as the beat of his heart. In addition, and this has been reported thousands of times, one or another of the Higher Initiates, or a fellow student, will be assisting the individual on the inner.

If we are doing it correctly, the individual's journey should symbolically resemble an iceberg. What is outwardly visible is only the tip, a tiny fraction of what is happening in the inner life. The chelas who have everything going on on the outside, who ignore the spiritual exercises, and have no inner life are headed for failure. They have joined an organization and have consumed themselves with busy work, talking, thinking, doing all the time . . . and no stillness. They talk about the Master constantly, but they never hear him. Every time he tries to get through to them he gets a busy signal. This frantic individual with no inner life is not following the path of Eckankar, regardless of what it looks like, and eventually it will catch up with him or her.

Well, you got this far. I'm assuming you've traced your journey, examined your crossroads, and you've already written a letter to the Living ECK Master or the International Headquarters. Among other things, you are sent an order form with which you may enroll in the study program. The first series of twelve monthly discourses is called *The ECK Dream Discourses*. In it the student, or chela, begins building the foundation of his own unique spiritual path. Also in this series are many techniques for the out-of-body and Soul Travel experiences.

If there is a class available to you, and you wish to augment your study in a group, you may do so. If there are no classes available, or that is not your preference and you will be studying by yourself, it is fine.

When Paul first wrote the discourses, there were no Satsang classes. All ECKists studied alone. It works fine both ways. Today's students are fortunate to have the option to also study with a group when they desire, but the wonderful part about it is that if, for some reason, one does not feel comfortable doing that, it is not necessary.

Over and over in Eckankar you will find this dynamic of personal choice or preference. There is a superstructure of sorts, but we each decide and create our own personalized path within the framework of the larger, outer path.

Attitude and Sunburn

There are several tips, as you take these first steps, I'd like to pass along to you that may make it a little easier and more comfortable. The first one is critical.

As you begin to study, and you get started on your spiritual exercises you may become excited, intense, and impatient to know all you can as fast as you can. Some people read every book they can get their hands on. They're doing their contemplation and reading their discourses. And all of a sudden they don't feel so well. They get nervous, experience anxiety, sometimes trembling. Often there are upsetting dreams or psychic aberrations, or the mind is jumping about crazily. This is a classic case of Spiritual Sunburn brought on by gluttony.

If this had happened to you from eating

too much food, a doctor would probably tell you to take an antacid and go to bed. When one overdoses spiritually, the Living ECK Master or the Higher Initiate will counsel you to "Stop everything!" Put away all your books, tapes and discourses. Stop the spiritual exercises. Often the physical discomfort is alleviated by a large dose of red meat. Buy yourself a steak and just put it all out of your mind until your body's vibrations level out. What you have done is raised your vibrations faster than your system can adjust.

The reason that the discourses of ECK are to be studied one per month is for your gradual unfolding. They are carefully geared and metered for the unfolding of what is called the Thousand Petalled Lotus. The layers must be slowly peeled away and in a natural progression. This process cannot be hurried. The system will balk. To use an analogy, if you were in the fifth grade, studying long division and fractions, or whatever it is they study now in the fifth grade, and a workbook on calculus fell into your possession, what could you do with it? The best you could do would be to toss it aside and say, "I'm not ready for that yet,

I'll get to it later." The worst you could do would be to read it, try to do the problems, fail, become upset and confused and give up math altogether.

If the student beginning *Satsang I* or the *Precepts* should find a copy of *The Master Discourses,* the discourses for Initiates, he would not understand what it was saying. This is not a matter of intelligence, but of the Thousand Petalled Lotus. The outer layers must come off first for the inner layers to have meaning. Patience. Oh, my friend, is that not your greatest challenge?

The principal difficulty surrounding gluttony and impatience is that the system, particularly the mental faculties, rebels. A certain concept, that had you opened to it gently would be perfectly clear, will strike you as ridiculous, untrue, or incongruous. The mind rejects, the Astral body becomes angry. The mouth, without the brain in gear, says, "Man—I'm not buying that!" But is that *you* saying that, or is it your entire system warning you that you're pushing too hard?

There is an easier way to do it. Pace yourself. Tune in to yourself. Don't force yourself to grapple with things that make you uncomfortable. You may have wondered about some of the odd behavior related earlier concerning my first year and a half in Eckankar. I read nothing that first year but my discourse once a month. No other ECK books. I did not want to meet other ECKists and certainly was not ready to accept the powerful figure of a personal spiritual guide into my life. This was my innate response to how much and how fast I could comfortably assimilate these teachings. That was what my instincts demanded of me. It is within each of us, this ability to pace ourselves and select the rôle that suits our individual needs.

When I wrote my first letter to Paul Twitchell, I made a deal with him. I would go along with him for awhile and see what he had to say, but I would not take *anything* on faith. He would have to prove it to me. I would have to experience a thing before I believed it. For my part, I promised him only one thing: An open mind. I thought I was being very tough. Little did I know, I'd just made Paul Twitchell his favorite kind of deal.

This is the way I kept my half of the bargain: When my monthly discourse arrived and I began to read the material, I did not approach it as we usually approach ideas. I was detached about each thing he presented. I did not think, "I can believe that is true," or "I don't believe that is true." The teachings were broken down into two categories: The things I knew, and the things I didn't know. That is all the comment I allowed my mind to make.

I remember particularly coming upon the doctrine of reincarnation. I did not, at that time, believe in reincarnation. Neither did I disbelieve it. I simply knew next to nothing about it. Perhaps I vaguely thought, as so many people do, that it had something to do with coming back as animals. But I really didn't KNOW, and when I came to it in my reading I said, "That is something I don't know," and went right on, not feeling obliged to think any more about it.

A long time went by. Then, amazingly, one morning I woke up and suddenly understood reincarnation. I *knew*. That was all there was to it. No experience. No discussion. No dramatic revelation. Just one day I didn't know it and the next day I knew it; I understood what he'd been talking about. How could this be? Simple. When I first came upon the information it was covered by other petals of the Lotus. Once they had fallen away, that petal was revealed. I did not have to work on reincarnation, I had to work on the things that held me from the knowledge of it. It was always mine, but I could not come to it before its time. This is the difference between "heart wisdom" and "head knowledge." So it is with every single facet of the path. This is the reason the Master warns the chela about asking too many questions. If you ask a question before its time, it is like a spoon in an empty bowl, it's useless. But a question whose time has come, voilà! The petal in front of it drops, and you have not the question, but the answer.

Quieting the mind means less thinking, calculating, judging, worrying, fearing, hoping, trying, regretting, controlling, jittering or distracting. The mind is still when it is totally here and now in perfect oneness with the action and the actor.

—W. Timothy Gallwey
The Inner Game of Tennis

3 Contemplation: Opening Night

Very soon after you begin these studies, you will be reading about the spiritual exercises and you'll find some simple directions as to how to go about it.

I can't stress enough the importance of daily contemplation. For some it is a difficult thing to arrange. Unless you've already been trained in yoga or meditation techniques, it's an uphill struggle, but it simply must become one of your top priorities for probably a thousand reasons which I'll try to condense to a few of the most important ones.

Primary and the toughest: You must get control of your mind. Sometimes people who already have an intense, active inner life, who have inner experiences all the time, think the exercises are not necessary to them. One person like this told me that she actually had so much inner life spontaneously that when she tried to do the spiritual exercises, it seemed to diminish what she was experiencing in her walking, talking, ordinary life. I suggested that she probably would benefit from the spiritual exercises as much as anyone else because in spite of her experiences, her mind would not allow her to have them when *she* decided to. In her case, the exercises were not for the experiences, but to gain control of the mind. Actually, she even needed to become proficient in gaining control over the inner experiences.

In spite of what is popularly believed by almost everyone, you are not your mind. Descartes, the famous French philosopher said, "I think, therefore I am." What poppycock! It goes like this: "I am, in spite of the fact that I think." You can think *something*, but you can Be anything or everything, including that which is unthinkable. When you have learned to get your mind under control, and you do this by stilling it in contemplation, you can have experiences of knowing, of depth and beauty for which you can find no thought or word. When you try to think of it, your brain is too puny, it cuts out like a computer with its plug pulled. When you try to describe it, you can find no words that come anywhere close. A whole new language would have to be invented. All you can say is, "I experienced. It's mine. It just is." It happened beyond your mind, and since you can't think it or say it, neither your mind nor anyone else's can attack it or take it away from you. But in your depths, you *know*. And you'll never forget.

Many individuals in Eckankar do not favor the lotus position for contemplation for several reasons, most notably because it has a long range effect on the circulation for many people, and prolonged use of it may result in passivity. The most common position recommended is sitting upright in a chair, both feet firmly planted on the floor and the hands in a relaxed position in the lap, eyes closed, but not tightly. Three deep breaths are taken and exhaled (or more if you really need to relax). The attention is placed on the *Tisra Til*, a point between the eyes at the base of the nose. Inside your head it feels a bit like you're cross-eyed at first, but later this sensation disappears completely. Now you begin to chant on your outflowing breath one of the words you've read in the books or discourses. Initiates of the second level and higher have their own personal charged word to do this. If you haven't come upon a word yet, try HU (pronounced as in *hu*man). You may roll this sound out, either silently or aloud in one long HUUUUUUUUUU all on the outgoing breath. It's better if you don't drag your breath out until you turn blue and lose consciousness. The trip you're taking should not be to the floor in a heap. Just flow that breath out until comfort asks that you stop and take a new one. Then repeat.

When you first begin, it's like driving a car. One has so many things to think about: The accelerator, the brake, the steering, the gears, the signals, and all those crazy drivers out there ready to do you in. We repeat and repeat the operation until all the little details become automatic and we no longer have to think of them.

How long you chant before you stop and let everything become silent varies among individuals. In the beginning, I was counting chants and going up to thirty or something. The problem with that is that all of these things engage your mind; keep it working in the process. And the purpose of the whole process is to get that little devil quieted down and out of the picture. So I recommend that you don't count. Just carry on for a few minutes until you're feeling pretty relaxed.

After awhile you'll get so you just know when to stop. Now comes the hard part. You stop chanting, you breathe naturally and easily. You keep the screen before you blank, avoiding all thoughts.

If you're average, right about now all hell is going to break loose. Your mind is going to be saying, "What's going on? What's happening? I don't see anything. I don't feel anything." Somewhere on your body, you'll feel an itch that wants to be scratched. Your bladder gets into the act and tells you you'd better get to the bathroom. The mind, uneasy about this attempt to put it in its place, will tell you to listen to that fly buzzing, or that hammer going outside. Don't be discouraged, you're normal. But you've got a picture of the task ahead of you, of how much you have to get control over.

Often what the beginning chela does not realize is that in deciding to do this thing, he has literally become a battlefield between the higher self, Soul, and the lower self, the physical organism. It is Soul that leads us into the contemplative state. Soul is saying, "Shut off all this noise and junk, and give me space to breathe, and grow, and experience." All this other "junk" has had control of the situation for a long, long time. It's not going to give up without a fight. It is right here, in the privacy of your own experience, that you will see how the lower worlds do not wish to let you go. It is here that you make your stand. You begin to make the shift in consciousness to the higher states.

Conceive of the word "I." Say, "I am Soul. I have a mind. I have a body. But the I who I am is Soul." It will help you in your contemplation if you immediately begin a strict discipline of your terminology. Never again get caught in the thought, "I have a Soul." Who is the "I" that has a Soul? This is an impossible statement. From now on when you say "I," you mean "I, Soul," and when you say, "I think," what you mean is, "My mind thinks," for you (and you know who that is) do *not* think. *You* perceive. You observe what your mind thinks.

Paul Twitchell has written that the mind is a good slave, but a poor master. True. Not only that, your mind can make you crazy. I realize that these words will offend a few of the intelligentsia. It's an unfortunate fact that the smarter you are, the harder you have to work at being Soul in control. It may be your badge of honor out in the world, but when you begin contemplation and you try to shut that thing up, you have twice as much work to do as your less complicated fellow being. In my files are lists of brilliant intellectuals, doctors, lawyers, engineers, accountants, writers, college professors... you name it. We have many of them in Eckankar, and they will tell you what a handicap their highly refined, intelligent minds were to them when they tried to touch down with that pure, sweet, true self within. But they did it. Each of them innately knew who they were, and they learned to suspend that valuable earthly commodity called "mind power" enabling them to touch base with the true self.

They are still brilliant and respected and functioning in their various fields—they have lost absolutely nothing, but they've gained a new dimension of awareness about who they are. And, if you have the opportunity, ask one of them. Their power and awareness and abilities in their lives have not decreased from these exercises in stilling the mind. They have increased dramatically. They now have access to insights, knowledge, and powers that the mind, alone, however well developed, cannot provide.

Although our first attempts to still our minds and bodies do create this battlefield effect, it is sometimes possible to ease that by giving reassurance and love to the whole organism. This is done by visualizing the entire self: Soul, body, emotions, mind, etc., as a microcosm. This entire creation is your own personal universe, a miniature replica of the greater universe—and you, Soul, are the god of this universe. Every atom, molecule and cell inside you is a tiny Soul in your care. They are serving you. And they do it extraordinarily well considering the fact that they seldom get any personal love and attention from you, and at times have even suffered insults and injuries due to your lack of consideration for them.

In a contemplative state, or even as you read along, visualize yourself as the microcosm. Since you are God here, and all this is your realm, you can visit any part of your realm merely by placing your attention there. Using visualization, or the imaginative faculty, go down inside your right foot. Not in your head. Inside. Be there. Look around. Journey around the muscles, tendons, bones. You can be anywhere in this universe of yours instantly by merely placing your attention there and by seeing yourself there. Switch quickly to the inside of your heart, then move around to the lungs. Travel inside your arm down into your hand. What does it look like from the inside?

On your mission as peacemaker, travel through all the parts of your universe. Thank all the cells and organs for the fine job they are doing in your behalf. Send to each, waves of love. This is your greatest creative power as Soul, as the god of this universe. Talk to everyone in the microcosm, informing them that some changes are coming; changes that will benefit each individually and the Whole. Give assurance and request cooperation. Once you get into your incredible journey and it becomes easier to see it, feel yourself doing it, visit the emotions, the psyche, and the mind. Let them all feel your good will and that they have nothing to fear.

As Soul, your attention is very much like a spotlight. Whatever you shine this light upon receives energy. The organs and cells of your body will benefit from this attention. And since you've made this journey of love and caring, your microcosm should be more cooperative, for you've made friends with it and demonstrated that you mean it no harm.

This exercise was recommended as a peacekeeping mission. It works quite well also for a general sense of well being. It can also be used to promote healing to a specific area. Certainly if you were able to accomplish it, you experienced the Soul-self in operation. More than that, you may be surprised to learn that you have just done that thing called Soul Travel. Were you under the impression you had to go "out" somewhere? Well, you did go out. Out of your mental body into your own personal universe. You have just explored one tiny area in that microcosm, the physical. But there is infinitely more to you, and your journeys are endless, because you are endless. If you want to "get out," may I suggest you consider "getting out inside"? Although you may not realize it at this moment, there is nothing out there in all creation that is not present in you, in your personal microcosm, which is an exact replica of the macrocosm.

If you want to experience out-of-body projection, to do what is sometimes called mind travel, to see or visit some place around the planet, you can get out. The chief benefit of doing this is that the awareness of the body and the grip of the mind has been overcome. One can leave it and come back to it unharmed. A new perspective about the experience called "death" is achieved. It is also a good lesson in the mechanics of letting go of the physical senses.

One morning, after a year or so of my studies in Eckankar, as I was in that twilight zone between sleep and consciousness, I felt myself drift out of my body and float around the room. Suddenly I realized what was happening. "Hey! I'm...." I started to think. But the second my mind thought about it, I was back in my body. I lay back, turned off my head and relaxed again, approaching the twilight area. Out I drifted again. Again I got excited, and again I snapped back into my body. I knew I was doing it, but I was trying to experience and record it with all my senses. It was all these guys wanting to be a part of it that kept snapping me back. If you want to project, you've got to keep the sharp senses out of it, because that's attention on the physical, and where your attention is, you are.

Another good example of projection is a common experience of musicians, conductors, and music lovers. Have you ever played or listened to a piece of music with such concentration that you lost all awareness of your body, of what time it was, and what place you were in? You were so into it that nothing existed but the music. In a way you were the music. The music was all there was. Well, you were "out," or "in," whatever term suits you. You were definitely not on this plane at the time. In fact the only time that existed was that in the space of the music.

Some people are able to do this while reading a book or watching a film. They get out of their body and into the action of the story. They are totally unaware of their surroundings.

For some students, things begin to happen in the first attempts at contemplation. Some actually "see" the sound they are chanting flowing out into the inner space. They put their attention, awareness, self, there and they ride on that wave of sound right off into the inner planes. Some have their mind screens fill with kaleidoscopic colors, moving and changing. Others will see a pulsating vortex, or other shapes that come and go, change and rearrange. Excitement has to be contained or the senses will take over and pull the plug. How can you help but get excited? Pretend you're not.

As you progress, you will see more and more on the screen. Happenings that are not creations of the mind at all. Whatever you are seeing, including the Master, will have a strange habit. If you look right at it, it will move off to the side, and if you follow it with your eyes it will eventually disappear completely. One holds them by "looking without looking." That is an oblique looking, or a peripheral looking. Later as you call less and less of your senses into the act, you will (as you explored your body) get right out into the space where they are, like Alice through the looking glass, and the real inner journeys begin. The blank mind screen eventually disappears and each time you contemplate, you are immediately looking where the blank screen used to be, at the door or opening into the inner worlds.

But for the beginner this door is usually blocked by his own habits, opinions, attitudes, fears, etc. One of the blocks a lot of us have to dissolve is the doubt that there is a door there at all. Ah, but it's there and thousands have found it, and so can you. How? You just go there every day, chant, still the senses and the mind—and wait. Each time you do this, it's like thick, black cobwebs slowly dissolving and parting. You don't have to do anything else, just keep at it and know that every attempt you make is bringing you closer. That open door is yours. Nothing can deny it to you if you keep at it.

The average contemplation is about thirty minutes. It could be more if you're having an experience and going with it. If you're still punching your way through the cobwebs and taming your body and mind, try for fifteen minutes. A chela once told me she simply could not sit still for more than five minutes. "Well then sit for five minutes," I said, "And gradually increase it another minute until you can handle thirty." She did that and it worked. You've got to sneak up on these things sometimes. Be creative.

Another complaint by some is that they can't get anywhere sitting in a chair. I suggest you try that awhile anyway. It may be your mind using that as a ploy and the name of the game is to show it who's boss. But if, after repeated attempts in the chair, you still find it doesn't suit you, try something else. Some prefer lying on the floor or on a bed (the advanced student can do this *anywhere*, including on a bus, or a plane, or in the dentist's chair). Some people are bedridden and have to do it lying down. There's nothing wrong with it, though many report they tend to fall asleep. However, as with most everything, for some there are different advantages to each method. One person told me that when she began contemplation in a chair, her body would shake and tremble. This was, no doubt, a combination of excitement, intense desire, and anxiety. She shifted to lying on the bed every afternoon. Immediately after her chanting she'd fall asleep. Twenty to twenty-five minutes later she'd awaken abruptly and instead of the lethargy and grogginess that usually followed an afternoon nap, she found herself energized, alert, and very refreshed. Whatever was going on there certainly benefitted her and some inner adjustments took place, because eventually she was able to recommence her exercises in the chair in a very relaxed and successful manner. Incidentally, a brief note about sleep: As in the above example, once the chela begins his or her studies, connects with the Master, and begins tuning into the Light and the Sound Current, a lot of important work is done in the so-called sleep state. Much of this work is the inner teachings and while there may not be conscious memory of what has gone on, there is change occurring and assistance being provided. Very often this is felt upon awakening with no specific recall as to why.

The important thing is to find what works for you. We are all individuals and *how* we do the contemplation doesn't matter nearly as much as *that* we do it. Don't be afraid to experiment. A friend of mine spent several of her early ECK years contemplating in a dark clothes closet. It's always an upsetting moment when one of us calls another on the phone and we find out we have interrupted their contemplation. But it's something else when your friend tells you she was sitting in the closet when you called.

Actually, this person was extremely sensitive to outside stimuli and the darkness helped her concentration. Some people have a problem with eyelid fluttering or are distracted by the amount of light that penetrates the eyelids. A sleep mask could be helpful, or try sitting at a table, placing the elbows on the table and the fingers pressed very gently across the eyelids.

There are many other facets to individual contemplation. If you've really worked at it, and nothing happens, you are, in some way, holding yourself back. But don't be discouraged. Seek out an ECK teacher (Arahata) or Higher Initiate and talk it over. They'll help you. If this is not possible, write to one, or to International Headquarters. Just don't give up. I've gone through many of the things we ordinarily have the student try who isn't having any results. However, I would venture to say that at least eighty percent of those who ask for help and complain about nothing happening in their contemplation, usually admit that they are not doing it on a regular basis. Without this practice being established, it isn't of much use to give out other suggestions, because there is no discipline involved. And discipline is the name of the game.

The day will come when you go inside, step out the door and you meet the Master. You may see him in white, or in color, or a ball of light, or you may not see him at all but feel his presence off to the side and a little in back of you. Often the Presence of the Master is experienced clear down to the physical body.

Although it's probably impossible at first, try not to get excited. Keep everyone in the microcosm on hold, and promise yourself an ecstatic celebration later, but for now, stay quiet, unemotional, and attentive. Let him show you or tell you what is next. Expect nothing except to follow his lead. Sometimes that is all that happens. He has shown you that he is there. You saw that and you felt that. Later, as you become more adept, you can sit at a table, writing or reading, or whatever, and in full consciousness tune in to that place where he positions himself in your microcosm and once again feel that presence. It differs in individuals but for me it is a place behind my right ear that extends down my back to the diaphram. When it happens, it feels somewhat warmer than the rest of me, and there's a small pressure as if I'm being lightly hugged.

Another reason that we need to go inside is to become proficient in the subtle experience; to be able to tune into the small, still voice within. Life is filled with choices and uncertainties for most of us. More often than not, when we are faced with choices, we will gravitate toward the ones that are safer and more pleasant (or the least unpleasant). The emotions prefer to be comfortable. The mind prefers the known to the unknown. The individual whose consciousness is cemented into the lower worlds will usually go for the *status quo*, and all his choices are limited to that range.

But the true spiritual seeker is an individual on the move. He has to grow. To experience. To change those things about himself that hold him back. This can most effectively be accomplished by inner direction. If you ask yourself the question: "What is the best possible direction for me to take in this situation?" The mind, the sub-mind, and the emotions, have their own patterns, habits, preferences. You've already seen how they've gone to work to mess up your contemplation. Are you going to trust them to make an important life-decision for you? Especially when you have access to your truest, wisest counsel? No, of course not. You go within, turn their noise and demands off, and in the silence, put your question to the Wise Ones of your universe: You, Soul, and the Inner Master. You will know.

Those who've been doing this for a period of time will tell you about the results. Sometimes the answer is what you were really wanting. This kind of answer cannot entirely be trusted, but if that's all you get, you have to go with it. Generally, when I get an answer that my human self prefers, I test it because it may be tainted by my desires. I will return to the inner several more times with the question. If the same answer always occurs, then I go with it.

The most rewarding and affirming experience, however, is when an answer comes that you were not expecting at all. Sometimes it's a choice the human self would not have preferred. Sometimes it's a whole new thing that hadn't ever been thought. Many answers are surprises. But the adept student trusts his inner advisor, and has learned through many testings not to question or chew it over endlessly, trying to understand the full ramifications of it with the mind. He follows it. And amazing things happen.

In the beginning one contemplates and learns to tune in on the inner direction. Later, you will become so used to this that you can do it anywhere, anytime, under any conditions. Furthermore, as Soul becomes the dominant factor and is accustomed to being in control, It can interfere on Its own right, right through the busy traffic of the mind and daily activity, to have a word with us when we need to do a certain thing, or stop doing something.

I have seen more than one Initiate, present company included, begin to say something and get stopped dead in their tracks. You're likely to hear this, "I just got stopped. I was about to say something I shouldn't say." It's a commonplace happening. To an outsider it probably sounds weird. But student-to-student such an experience is understood and treated with respect (although sometimes you're dying of curiosity, wondering what the forbidden statement might have been).

If it weren't for my ability to drop the physical world and go to the inner worlds, you and I would not be together in the experience of this book. There would be no music composed, poems written, or paintings done. Or if there were, it would be *terrible* stuff.

If I haven't given you sufficient reasons to do your daily contemplation, you may want to reconsider your commitment. The difference between those who contemplate and those who don't is about the same as the difference between an ice cube and an iceberg. You might make it without contemplation, but I'd be less than honest if I didn't tell you your chances range from slim to zero.

*True genius resides in the capacity
for evaluation of uncertain, hazardous
and conflicting information.*
—Winston Churchill
1874-1965

*The opposite of a correct statement
is a false statement. But the
opposite of a profound truth may well be
another profound truth.*
—Niels Bohr
1885-1962

4 The Plot Thickens: Paradox Island

We had a busy night last night. When I awakened the word "paradox" was in my mind. "Yes," I thought, "the paradox is a subject I should write about to you."

As you progress in your studies, at some point the paradox will overwhelm your consciousness. It is a word, a thing, a place, a state of consciousness. You may experience this as a brief interlude or you may mess around with it for a protracted time. Since the Mental Plane was a pretty foreign place to me, I hung around in there on Paradox Island for weeks on end. It went like this: Whatever occurred to me, or was said to me, or I read, had its opposite counterpart which was also true and it would immediately flash in on me. For the nearly four weeks I was on the island, I was practically immobilized. I couldn't do anything because the minute I had a reason to do it, I also had a reason not to do it. And vice versa.

I didn't like it much. An hour with it would have been sufficient for my taste, but apparently I was not to be let out of it until I got the message. By the time I was released I was feeling like my brain was fried, but I did understand that one can encompass contradictions without the slightest discomfort.

As the Petals of the Lotus unfold, you will come upon this one called Paradox—and it will be the experience of it. But right now, let's go into the idea of it, because it may ease the inner tensions somewhat.

Somewhere in my voluminous reading I came across an idea that utterly fascinated me; it really struck an inner chord. Essentially it was this: Whenever you look at something in the physical world, you are seeing only one half of it. Its other half is invisible. After I got going on it, I realized that this is just another way of saying what is said in many different ways throughout the ECK teachings. It just happened that that particular way of saying it unlocked one of my doors. I Soul Traveled for days on this concept of the invisible half.

I tried to envision something: a tree, my coffee cup, a painting, a book, as its whole self, that is both its manifested and unmanifested halves. About now the mind may cut out, you may have to "perceive" to stay with me. No matter what whole thing was envisioned, I came to a circle. And within the circle is everything: positive/negative, form/formless, yin/yang, the Microcosm. When I got to that point, I Soul Traveled for days on the circle. It is impossible for me to put into words what I saw about the circle. But I can tell you it's a key. Hold it with the deepest respect, and whenever you come upon it in your reading, or spiritual exercises, or dreams, be aware that you are touching upon one of the great mysteries of existence.

What has the circle to do with the paradoxes? Everything. What we are about here in Eckankar is the expansion of consciousness. Although you will see charts of the planes and the God Worlds depicted in a vertical fashion, and you will hear terms such as "higher initiations" or "down here in the physical," "up there in the higher worlds," all of that can be misleading. We are not going from here to there. We are spreading out, from here, encompassing ever more; an awareness or realization, if you will, of what is. This expansion occurs in ever widening concentric *circles*. Actually it's spherical.

That is why, in the strictest sense, on the path of Eckankar you are not learning something new, you are unfolding and expanding into what you always were. That is why there are times when you come across a certain piece of information and although it may be totally foreign to anything you've been taught in this life, you have the sensation that you are remembering something you knew but had forgotten.

In the process of this concentric traveling, which comes about through your discourses and contemplation, at times you will experience states of knowing which you enjoy but can't hold on to. You stretch out and then you come back, much like a rubber band. Don't be discouraged. Keep on plugging. Because every time you stretch out, a little of the tension in that rubber band leaves, and although you seem to be back to a normal state, you are a little wider in consciousness. You may not notice or feel the change, but it's with you. I heard this rubber band analogy that first night I saw and heard Paul talk. (You see how that was? No matter how I was resisting him, he was getting the message over.) When he talked about the rubber band, he said this:

"I'm going to keep stretching you and stretching you, until all the stretch has gone out and you won't snap back anymore."

I'd like to insert an aside in here concerning drugs. It is possible to achieve some degree of altered states, and expansion through chemicals. Let's don't kid ourselves. Why do you think people are doing it? I'll spare you a corny lecture on chemical residues, and the danger of exploring areas you haven't achieved by developing spiritual stamina and a natural adjustment of the system's vibratory rate. An excellent book on this subject is "The Master Game" by Robert S. De Ropp. Dr. De Ropp is a biochemist, but he moves from physiology to the higher states and gives an excellent explanation of why a master is necessary.

I'll give here two reasons why the expansion of consciousness through the natural means taught and guided by the ECK Masters is far superior to the chemically induced "high."

The bad news is this: In the chemical high one not only snaps back, but there is frequently a "slingshot" effect. We can, in returning to the normal state of consciousness, come down, further down than we were before we began. This can result in depression, anxiety, and an inability to cope.

The second reason is so obvious that it probably goes without saying, but I will anyway. Every time the person who uses drugs wants to have an experience he/she has to find and take more dope. All I have to do is find a quiet corner and close my eyes. And every time I come back, a little more of the snap is out.

In line with these other methods of opening and expanding the consciousness, a friend of mine who has studied it extensively brought up the subject of using the Kundalini method, and I thought I'd mention it briefly. While Kundalini can open and expand, it can also be extremely dangerous. It can be worse than a negative hallucinogenic drug experience and could be permanently damaging. One of the books Paul Twitchell recommended in his reading list is *Cosmic Consciousness*. This book goes into the problems associated with Kundalini Yoga, including the story of one person who went completely insane. I don't believe there are any masters working to open the Kundalini forces in the old Kundalini method in this day and age. If so, they are not true masters. These methods just aren't necessary anymore.

Until you have stretched into the paradoxes, which merely means you are able to encompass contradictions without discomfort, you may find your mind blowing an occasional fuse over some of the things you come across in the writings of Eckankar. You will come upon references and teachings from other systems and religions. You will find the Masters saying things in many different ways. All of them will not be for you, but somewhere in there will be a key for you that opens new doors. I read, for instance, that what is in this world is but a reflection of what is in the other worlds. I read, "As above, so below." Not much happened. But when I read about the invisible half, I was on my way. Everyone will not respond to that as I did. But it is in there somewhere for each individual, and in order for that to be so, contradictions are necessary. If you are in earnest about this journey, don't worry about the contradictions and the references to other systems and beliefs. There are a few groups and individuals out there in the world who would rather none of us made this journey. They are worrying day and night about such things. Since they're perfectly willing to worry about all that at no charge and with no desire to progress beyond it, why not let them do it for you? And we will get on with the business of Soul.

Let's play with another analogy.

We have a large, beautiful German Shepherd named Micha. The German Shepherd is a working dog; that is its nature. The problem at our house is there isn't much work for Micha to do. No one here is blind, there's no police work to be done, and she doesn't believe in barking at people and scaring them because she adores human beings.

So there she is, a working dog with no job to do. But Micha is very bright. She invented a job. She catches flies.

Have you ever seen a German Shepherd working? It's a marvelous thing to behold. All the senses are a hundred percent on alert. The ears are pointed forward, like radar scopes, to catch the tiniest sound. The eyes are intense. The body is taut; the muscles seem to enlarge to twice their size. The dog patrols back and forth, missing nothing. It digs in and springs with a speed and power that is awesome. Micha does all this in the process of catching flies. She loves this work and she is deadly serious about it. Her pride in herself and her pure joy in her work is a sight to behold. And when she has caught one, she is ready to be congratulated and praised. She loves this so much in fact that she's expanded her job to include bees, grasshoppers, dragonflies, and butterflies. But for those of you whose sensibilities flinch at the idea of the wasting of even one of God's tiny creatures, let me assure you that Micha is quite adjusted to the agony of defeat. She rarely hits on one, they are too fast for her. That's not the point of it. This is a job; a service she is performing for her owners.

Once we understood what this strange behavior was about, that the dog needed to work, we hired a trainer and put her through Obedience Training. Now when she builds up steam we are able to put a leash on her and give her commands which she follows to the letter. Micha adores this work even more than chasing insects. She knows the drawer where her leash is kept and when she wants to work, she'll put her nose to the drawer and make noises that mean, "Let's get going, folks!"

It struck me that Micha is a wonderful

analogy for the mind, and particularly for the areas we are now discussing. As Micha is a dog whose nature is to work, so is the mind a tool whose nature is to work. As we become the master of this tool, it does the work that we command it to do. When we have not yet encompassed Paradox Island, and we have not yet put the mind through Obedience Training, the mind in its desire to always be working, will attack the contradictions and the similarities and all sorts of other things, just as Micha gleefully attacks the insects.

Here are a few examples of fatal mind attacks: Joe Doakes signs up for a series of discourses. He reads them, plus several books, for six months or so. Joe has read a lot of Eastern thought, and he comes upon passages that ring a bell. "I know what this is: it's nothing more than warmed over Hinduism." He writes his local travel agent and cancels his journey.

At the same time, on the other side of town, Floyd Flak has been reading the discourses too, and several other books. What Floyd sees are references and thought patterns that he came across years ago in Theosophy. "Ah, I know what this is. It's nothing more than warmed over Theosophy." He, too, cancels his journey. Floyd and Joe are gone now. They got it all figured out; all solved and explained away. Since they are very proud of how clever they are, if you happen to meet one of them, they'll be more than happy to explain it all to you. They'll particularly enjoy showing you Paradox Island. Of course they have totally missed the point, which is, that in the written material of Eckankar you will find similarities here and there to every religion, science, and belief system on the planet, and a whole lot from other places. This is because in his training for the task ahead of him, Paul Twitchell studied every religion, science, and belief system he could find on the planet, and a whole lot from other places. In this process he found the universal thread and he laid it out there for us so that he could meet each individual on his home ground, regardless of what that is. Gradually, and carefully over a period of time he shows you where that fits in with the Whole, in the universal scheme. This, to me, is one of the most interesting aspects of Paul's work. His detractors point to this facet of his work and make the claim that Eckankar is really a synthesis of a lot of things. The student who has successfully carried out the work and has traveled into the other worlds, who has proven by his or her own experience that the path is valid, understands the universal thread. A case can be made for both points of view; however one is mental and the other is experiential.

Come with me on a little trip. Let's peek in on Paul Twitchell doing his work. We enter his study and we see a giant form bent over a work table. He is putting together what seems to be a huge jigsaw puzzle. Each piece is intricately shaped and labeled. This one says Christianity, another Buddhism, there's Hinduism, Zen, Islam, Judaism, Rosicrucians, Scientology, Astrology, Geometry, Psychology, Spiritualism, Zoroastrianism, and so on. Slowly, carefully, piece by piece he puts them together until there is one great picture for us to see.

And as we watch him do this, we are giants with him. When we zoom in on this picture, we see it as a living thing. Every piece is populated with its believers and proponents. Hey, this is a good show. Look at all the people on those pieces. They're arguing and fighting with each other, each claiming their piece is the right piece, the only true piece.

We stand here with Paul Twitchell looking down at this puzzle he's put together and we see that the people down there, clinging tightly to their chosen pieces of the puzzle, are very short. They can't see very far in any direction. They can see their closest neighbors and they're aware of the taller ones over there who are making so much noise, but they can't see that they're all locked together in one master plan, and they have no idea of how many others there are, or of the size, shape and nature of these other pieces. Oh, some of them vaguely know some of those others exist, but they write them off as unimportant and/or misguided. Most of the people, however, are so absorbed in their own particular piece that they don't believe it's a piece. They stand on their tiny segment and they talk to each other and they say things like, "This is it. This is all there is."

So here we are, you and me and Paul, looking down at what he's put together for us. And we can see down there the piece or pieces of the puzzle that we used to occupy. And we remember what we used to think and say, and we laugh. Wait. Wait a minute. Stop laughing and look down at that little piece over there.

There's Floyd Flak and Joe Doakes telling everyone around them on that piece how they got it all figured out. Well, look closer. There are people all over the puzzle loudly proclaiming that Eckankar is really their piece of the puzzle. Come to think of it, since Eckankar encompasses all life, they are correct in a sense.

Just before we leave this room that holds the big picture of all the teachings and ideas that span the centuries of civilization, I want to share something else with you. As you hovered over the puzzle with all its pieces fitted together, did the question come to you, "Is this big picture I'm looking at Eckankar?" The answer is no. What you're looking at is the introductory material.

Behold! human beings living in an underground den...they see only their own shadows, or the shadows of one another, which the fire throws on the opposite wall of the cave.

—Plato
c. 428-348 B.C.

5 The Program vs. Programming

I figured today we'd move on to something else, but found myself held to my analogy of Micha and the mind. A good analogy is like a beautiful, multifaceted crystal. You can hold it and turn it over and find it works in many directions that weren't obvious at first. Let's turn this one over and see what else it can say to us.

There are many cults proliferating these days. They, too, fit into the big puzzle and they attract people who need to have their particular kind of experience. When we read or hear about some of these cults, we often feel that their belief systems are bizarre. Sometimes it's hard to figure out why anyone would go for that kind of a trip. Obviously they answer some need in the individual which is not being met.

Many of the people who are drawn to the cults, such as the Reverend Jim Jones', are people who are very frightened by life. They feel their lives are out of control and there is nothing they can do about it. They are looking for a Daddy (or

Mommy) to take care of things, to take responsibility for them and make all their decisions for them. They are ripe little plums ready for the picking by the charismatic cult leader. They can't wait to find someone to take the burden of self-responsibility from their shoulders. This kind of abdication of responsibility for one's own life is as close as one can come to being a walking, talking suicide.

This type of individual, incidentally, is not necessarily confined to the cults. I once had a neighbor who was this type and she was a Roman Catholic. She turned to her parish priest for every single decision that affected her life. She simply couldn't function without running to him to check out what was the "right" thing to do. I don't know if this particular priest enjoyed the fact that the woman was only a puppet in her own life and he was pulling all the strings, or if he was merely caught in a situation he couldn't see his way out of. Whatever the case, had she not found this way in the church, she'd have ended up with some charismatic cult leader, a psychic reader, or some other person who would tell her what to do. The mind we're looking at here doesn't even fit into the analogy of the working dog. If this mind is analogous to any dog, it's one who's been hit by a car and is lying paralyzed and unconscious in the street. This system is totally operated by the emotions—and someone else's mind.

The cults that are really dangerous, though, are the ones that take a perfectly healthy, working mind and brainwash it. This is generally accomplished in an isolation-type environment and includes emotional and sensory deprivation, repetitive, hypnotic-type suggestions that gradually become locked in, and the "hostage syndrome." How can this work? Because the people who do that kind of thing understand quite well that the mind is a tool and like the working dog, it can be trained. Reduced to its lowest common denominator, it can think, but it cannot think for itself. Like a dog it can be used and abused and manipulated into crazy and weird places. The good news is, it won't last forever. No matter what has happened to that mind, there is a Soul in there observing what is being done. It may not be in control at the moment, but it's watching and learning and gathering experience—and its day will come.

It's very important that we get up above all this and get the overview. We need to see where it fits in the scheme of things. It seems to be a fine line to some people. What I'm trying to get over here is that once you see it in the overview, you see it's not a fine line at all.

As you travel this journey of this ancient teaching of Eckankar, it is *you* who gets control over your mind. It is you who are working constantly to achieve the ultimate harmony of your entire microcosm, with you, Soul, in control. As you progress, you will grow ever stronger in your willingness to be totally responsible for your every thought, word and deed. In the beginning you will have fellow students, teachers, Higher Initiates and the Masters standing by to assist you if you need it. But you have only one goal: To evolve into your own Mastership; to one day become the Co-worker with those wise and ancient Great Ones.

Before we leave the subject of the mind, there's one other thing that should be said about it. As long as you are here in this body, you will have to contend with this mind. Once you have gained control of it and have made it your servant and not your master, do not, I beg you, fall into complacency. I think St. Exupery was talking about the mind and the emotions when he wrote about the Little Prince keeping daily watch over and sweeping out his volcano. The Little Prince tells us his volcano is extinct; then he says, "But you never really know about volcanoes, do you?"

No matter how far you have traveled, how much awareness and insight you've encompassed, how many initiations you've gone through, don't turn your back on your volcano. I've seen some very advanced students of long standing and great accomplishments drop their guard and suddenly succumb to a fatal mind attack. This can be rather confusing and somewhat disturbing to the newer students (and even some of the older ones). What happens is a whole epidemic of mind attacks. It goes like this: "If they got that far and had all that awareness, how come they didn't see the trap?" Well, it's not so hard to understand if you look it over carefully. You're on the move. You're having experiences all the time. You're stretching and growing into all kinds of new awareness. What is your mind doing all this time? Is it out in a field somewhere smelling the flowers while you're doing all this work? Far from it. A lot of what you're doing is filtering back to it. It is indexing and filing information at an incredible rate. So as you grow more into your awareness of what is, your mind is also increasing in its complexity and its ability to be subtle and clever.

Every one of us would feel fortunate to get through a day in which we came to something important and the mind didn't try to seize it, lay claim to it and say, "You didn't get that, that came from my brilliant apparatus."

The further you go, the trickier and more subtle the tests become. There is a critical point for the Higher Initiate when he/she must pass through the eye of the needle. There can be no baggage on this passage, most particularly the mind and the ego. I'm throwing metaphors at you right and left, but it's easier to visualize these things metaphorically. Anyway, you get the idea of the difficulties involved. And that's all you or I can do, is get an idea. What it's really like, what the individual is actually going through we cannot know. It is presumptuous of us to make a judgment about it. All we can really do is stand aside and have respect for the test in progress, and take great care that we don't get sucked into something that really has nothing to do with us, lest somebody else's test suddenly becomes ours.

In the course of your studies you will continually run into references to "cause and effect." This is, possibly, the most important and the most often misunderstood principle you will have to deal with.

Gaining mastery over the mind, the ego, the emotions, is a necessity. To achieve higher states of consciousness, to operate from this position of Soul-in-control, really means we cease to be motivated by or the unconscious effect of the mind, emotions, etc. We become Cause. And when we *are* effect, we are knowing effect.

I don't know why it happens, but now and again I've seen students seize upon a concept or a principle as if they were Tarzan with a vine in his hands, and they swing out on that principle to its furthest 180 degree extreme. They may cut themselves off from their emotions to the point of feeling absolutely nothing, so that there is no room for any other reality except for God, whatever that is. They believe that their humanness, their delight, pleasure and pain in the simple experiences of everyday living and loving must go—and they turn their backs on the world and no longer relate to themselves as being in it. They sometimes express contempt for their body, for working and supporting themselves, for close relationships with other humans. They are trying to *escape* being the effect of anything.

This is not what the Masters are asking of us. On the contrary, the person who abdicates in this manner is not being cause at all, but rather is being the effect of an idea—and is not using his or her tool kit. Indeed, they've swung across the river, and are hiding out on a ledge on the other side of life. They've missed the point entirely. Eckankar is a Way of Life, not a way to avoid it. Maybe we are not *of* it, but we are *in* this world—and for a reason.

A very dear friend recently discussed this subject with me. He is one who swung out over the river and perched on a ledge for many years. He's come back now and is beginning to experience life and himself as a totality. He's a brilliant intellectual; a highly educated and gifted individual. He told me that he finally understood that in doing what he did, he had not learned to overcome being the effect of his emotions, but rather he'd hidden away from them, walled himself off, so that he simply didn't have to test himself.

He finally came off his ledge and he dove headlong into the river of life. He's in the process of discovering his God-self in the midst of his humanity. Everything about him is energized and electric. Life is new. He's discovering the simple thing he'd left out of the equation: Self-Realization does not occur when any part of the self has been condemned, feared, or walled off.

Self-Realization precedes God-Realization, and in order to achieve it, everything about us, all components, must be seen and understood with acceptance and harmony. Total harmony in the microcosm cannot occur in the presence of self-condemnation or self-rejection. This is not to say that we always need to indulge our baser instincts or our darker side, but rather we acknowledge they exist and are just as much a part of us as our higher instincts. I have seen people deny their human sexuality because they fear if they acknowledge it, it will get totally out of control. And perhaps they are right. But I have a serious question about the lesson of walking the middle path, about achieving one's goals, with such unresolved fear. Sexuality, the mind, the ego, the emotions are part of us. If they are unimportant, why are we here in the human form? There must be a purpose for us to have all these factors or we wouldn't have them.

I don't know, as yet, the answer, but have a hunch. I think they are modes of expression in a balanced state. It is only when they are karmically unbalanced they are exhibited in the extremes: Compulsive, addictive overindulgence or complete avoidance due to fear. In either instance, there are lessons on the agenda for neither state is being Cause; both are reactive states.

Let me use the emotions as an example of the misunderstanding that often occurs. The astral or emotional body is the next vibratory rate to the physical body. It is said to be part of what is called "the lower self." Many people are entirely run by an overindulged, overgrown emotional body, the most powerful aspect of which is fear. This individual can be, and is, manipulated by practically everybody and everything. Politicians, governments, religions, advertising agencies, canned music, husbands, wives, children, bosses; all use their knowledge of these fear levels to get the individual to operate in accordance with their wishes. Would you believe me if I told you that you can even trace ads for underarm deodorants and tooth paste to being basically geared to fear levels? This individual is the *unknowing effect* of his emotions.

Let's take the other side now. On the night of September 17, 1971, my phone rang at 1:00 a.m., awakening me from a deep sleep. It was a Higher Initiate calling me from Cincinnati informing me that Paul Twitchell had just died, translated from this plane, and she was asking me to please get in touch with Paul's wife, Gail and tell her. For a minute I was stunned. Then as I sat and thought about it, I realized that Paul had been trying subtly to prepare me for the fact that his earthly existence was about to terminate. I thought about the letter that had come a week and a half before with a lock of his hair enclosed, and a strange, cryptic message about what I was to do with it after he was gone.

I thought about the phone call, the night before he left for Cincinnati. He was grumbling about the trip, saying he was tired and really didn't feel like going. I said, "Paul..." and then suddenly a plug was mysteriously pulled in my head. Whatever it was I was thinking and feeling and about to say was wiped so totally out of my mind, so completely erased, that I just stood there mute and blank. There was a long silence between us, and then he said, "What were you about to say, Patti?" I laughed in confusion. "I don't know, Paul. It's the funniest thing, I had something important I wanted to tell you and it's just gone. It's left me completely." He laughed, too, and we talked some more, kidding gently, then said goodbye. It was the first and the last time Paul Twitchell ever called me in the evening.

I sat on the bed remembering the strange erasure of my thoughts—and suddenly knew what it was I had been going to feel and say, and was not allowed to. I also realized that on some level, he knew—and that the emotions had to be overridden—even his own. I once heard the ridiculous accusations that Paul Twitchell had committed suicide. I don't know where people dig up some of these absurd notions. It took all the strength and powers Paul could muster just to stay alive the last year or so of his life. He didn't have to do anything to translate, but he had to do more than any of us can even conceive of to stay alive as long as he did.

I concentrated on dialing Gail. My emotional body was in deep pain about the task. How do you tell a beloved friend that her husband has just died a continent away from home? I worked hard at controlling the pain and anxiety and keeping myself balanced. The phone rang and rang. She wasn't home.

I didn't know it at the time, but Gail had gone camping in the mountains with friends and wouldn't be home until morning. I sat up the rest of the night, trying to reach her every half hour. Each time I dialed, I went through the same sickening emotional keying up, only to have to give it up as there was no answer. In effect, emotionally, I went through the experience of telling Gail about twenty times, but all the pain was for Gail, or seemed to be. I hadn't allowed myself anything personally.

Finally in the morning Gail called me and I got it over with. Now it was time to think about myself. I thought about Paul and how tired he was. He'd been hanging onto and running a body that by rights should have stopped running a year before when he was poisoned by a demented man in Spain. He was ready to go, I think he wanted to go, but he had some things he just had to get finished first. He had told me in August, just a month before, that everything was going to be okay. He looked at me with total weariness and said, "You have no idea what a struggle it's been." I really didn't know exactly what a struggle it had been, but I knew a lot from the look of weariness on his face and the fatigue and resolution in his voice. I was glad for him that he could finally let go.

But there was something else that needed to be taken care of. The ascension of a Master is a joyous thing. It is impossible to be sad about it. But, I, Patti, had just lost a close, personal friend. Never again would I hear the phone ring and hear the soft, southern accent saying, "Well, Miss Patti, what's new?" Whatever marvelous things were going on out there in the universes with the Great Ones and the Masters of the Vairagi, couldn't change the fact that the most beautiful human being I had ever known in my life, my friend, was no longer here in my physical life, and I was going to miss him terribly. I allowed the tears to come and the pain of the loss to wash over the person, Patti. I cried for me. It was true. It was kind. It was necessary. This is an example of being the knowing effect of the emotions.

The advanced student is not afraid to experience the emotions. He or she understands them to be energy responses, and if they are appropriate to the occasion, they are experienced; allowed to wash through and pass away.

The Master, the Higher Initiates, still experience moments of anger. We, hopefully, just don't act out of it. The farther one goes in the initiations, the more one is aware of the power of one's anger, and great care is taken not to direct this at any individual. I know of one Higher Initiate who was being harassed by an individual to the end of their patience. When the straw that broke the camel's back happened—the arrival of a really insulting, degrading letter, the initiate, feeling the anger boiling to the red line, jumped in a car, tore down to the ocean, and dumped it all into the sea, rather than turn it on the persecutor. But after awhile, a lot of things that were once important cease to be, or are definitely not worth becoming upset over. If, however, they need to be handled and a clear message delivered, one actually will mock up anger that isn't really there and has absolutely no energy whatsoever, but sometimes a good dramatic effect.

To gain further insights into the tests that accompany the purification of the Higher Initiate, the lessons in power, ego, anger, etc., I highly recommend a study of the life of Milarepa.

Before we get to the end of this series of letters, I will share with you a formula which I guarantee will get you through these kinds of tests, any test. On the surface it looks ridiculously simple; in its inner essence it *is* simple. But not so easy. Paul told me about it when I was in one of my periods of inner turmoil and rebellion. Can you guess what it is? Stay tuned.

*The Devil would be the best way out
as an excuse for God...But even so,
one can hold God responsible for the
existence of the Devil.*
—Sigmund Freud
1856-1939

*A great many people think they are
thinking when they are merely
rearranging their prejudices.*
—William James
1842-1910

6 The Bad Guys and
The Good Guys

All night long we were going through the subject of the Kal. I'm having some difficulty working out what to say about it. When the subject came up, I saw something I hadn't consciously thought about before. That is that the newer students are working overtime on this differentiation between negative and positive, the Kal and the ECK. Sometimes it looks like a giant, cosmic Super Bowl. Sides have been chosen up and everyone, everything has its label, and we cheer and yell and root for the ECK and hiss, boo, sneer and condemn the Kal.

The thing I saw that I hadn't thought about before is that somewhere along the way I gradually stopped thinking about life in those terms. Nor could I recall hearing these phrases in any conversations with my fellow Higher Initiates since I can remember. This was an astonishing observation. I traveled around in it and explored it for the remainder of the night.

I should have known I was going to pull this thing out of the attic and air it out in the sunshine. There was a preview of it a few weeks ago. For the most part, I haven't been working with the chelas in the field on a one to one basis for many years, that is, in the outer world. Recently I began to do this again in my local area and I had this experience:

A woman called me, quite upset because she had done a dramatic reading and one of the chelas had made the statement to her, "Well, that's pretty Kal." She was quite distraught and wanted me to hear the tape and give her my opinion. Unable to imagine what obscenity this gentle Soul could have perpetrated I was intrigued and agreed to give it a listen.

We sat at my kitchen table, I adjusted my judicial robes, and she turned on the tape recorder. For the next ten minutes I sat enchanted. Waves of goose flesh rippled over me as I listened to the work and expression of a Soul in motion, struggling, questioning, hurting, soaring and growing. It was the saga of one turning ever upward and onward. Beautiful. It was very moving.

"So what do you think? Do you think it's too Kal?" she asked. I was totally perplexed. "I don't think it's Kal at all.

It's absolutely wonderful."

And so we began to dig down and under. What had elicited this comment from the other chela? Finally we saw it. It was the drama, the emotional pain that sometimes comes in the struggle to know and to grow and to go on. And *everybody* knows that emotions are Kal. In addition to that, the experience that was the subject of the artistic expression occurred before the woman found the outer path. At the least it was suspect.

I found myself utterly annoyed. (In the old days I would have said I was angry, but that was before I found out that anger is you-know-what. Now I just get utterly annoyed.) I was not annoyed at the chela who made the statement, I was utterly annoyed at the viewing of everything we perceive in such black and white fashion and then attaching labels to them.

I would like to meet the chela who made his/her way from there to here, who was able to accomplish that without an ounce of pain. I would like to meet the chela who thinks everything in their life B.E. (Before ECK) was of the Kal and everything after is of the pure, positive God Worlds. We need to sit down and have a long talk. And, you know, it wouldn't be so bad if they thought this way and kept quiet, because they'll grow out of it eventually. But to *say* it to or about another Soul, well, it utterly annoys me and it should you, too.

We should keep in mind that when we label anything, all such statements are value judgments, and unless they are made from the position of God-Realization, they are subject to the limitations of the plane and the level of consciousness from which they are made. Therefore, the most we can think or say about anything and be accurate is: "That is how it seems to be from this particular vantage point." And if our ego is out of the way, we are acutely aware of the fact that there are 359 other vantage points besides the one we are presently occupying. So having opinions and making value judgments about what somebody else is doing or saying is a pastime we are better off indulging in in silence, if we must indulge in it at all.

But, let me tie up a little loose string. Perhaps you caught it as it went by. I wrote "Unless a value judgment is made from the position of God-Realization, it is limited to..." If God-Realization is 360 degrees, and is the awareness of all, visible and invisible, encompassing the paradoxes, then everything has its purpose and its season and it is what it is. Its ISNESS is the function it is serving and it does that perfectly when all is known. If we look at it from a mental view, it seems to be imperfect. If we see it from 360 degrees, we see it is perfectly imperfect. From the viewpoint of God-Realization, labeling anything is impossible. You have had your moments when you've known this. Well, now you have an idea how far you were stretched.

We can't live, even the greatest of us, in that consciousness twenty-four hours a day. But even the newest beginner can help him/herself along with a little behavior modification. We start with our prejudices and our strong opinions, all that junk that was hanging off of me the first night I heard Paul Twitchell. Not only is the southern accent now music to my ears, but I'm not even mad at Lyndon Johnson anymore. Time and a lot of experience turned all that around 180 degrees for me. You can dig all these things out, one by one, by their roots. That's the hard way. There's an easier way. Maybe you'd like to try it.

We begin by assuming that there is

more to everything and everyone than is being manifested. Nothing is so poor, so imperfect, and so inadequate that it doesn't have something to teach us. Everything, everyone we see, has something for us if we could see them as they really are and not as they seem to be. Micha is "only a dog." That is the lowly category we have assigned to her. But Micha is a living, walking, breathing example of unconditional love. She communicates this to me constantly. In this respect, she is my master and I, her pupil. Right now, she loves everybody, because she totally loves and trusts my husband and me, and she figures people are people. But believe it, if someone came in here and tried to hurt me, she would try to kill them. Her love for me is so total that she wouldn't hesitate a second to lay down her life for me if the issue came up. Paul has said it is possible to experience God-Realization by looking deeply into the heart of a flower. If a flower or a dog can hold a key, what about your fellow man?

A good exercise in behavior modification in terms of dumping my attitudes and prejudices and assigning limits to the various creatures, including *homo sapiens* that I encountered, evolved from my reading about The Silent Ones; those giant, ancient Souls who work behind the scenes furthering the development of Souls on their journeys.

When I read that these spiritual giants will sometimes take on the forms of the physical world to effect some kind of exchange with its inhabitants, I was electrified. Immediately I flashed back to the dove in the Japanese park and the strange exchange that passed between us. Could it have been...? Who can say no? Paul mentioned a beggar approaching him for a coin for a cup of coffee. The beggar turned out to be anything but a beggar.

I believed and still do that this goes on. It changed me profoundly. To this day I always automatically include this possibility when I share an exchange with a stranger.

Another couple, Archie and Tom, and I both had simultaneous experiences with strange, white cats who came to stay for awhile at our houses; cats who exhibited very odd behavior towards us, and then abruptly disappeared.

The one who came to my house was a huge, fat tomcat. He followed me everywhere outside and when I was inside he'd run around the house peeking in the windows and watching me. He talked to me constantly in long, rolling mews. I don't know how to say it except that the cat had a "presence." It was comforting, reassuring, and somewhat spooky.

Enter Sandra, another Higher Initiate. She sees this visiting cat and she, too, feels there is something very unusual about it. Since I had exhausted every avenue in trying to find its owners, and I couldn't keep it indefinitely, and it showed no signs of leaving, Sandra agreed to give it a home. Not quite understanding why, I hung up from talking to Sandra and went out and told the cat what was going on and reassured him that he would love Sandra. I felt silly. Was he listening and understanding? I guess so. The next morning he was gone. I never saw him again. But some very special things happened in my life in the month or so that he was here, including a move on my part that resulted in the karmic resolution of an unhappy personal relationship.

Meanwhile, Tom and Archie's white cat was sitting at the foot of their front porch. He seemed to be guarding the place. He sat there day and night. He was very strange and different; Ascetic, a thin, pale, frail-looking cat, with intense eyes. He sat there for weeks, rarely eating. He never moved, even when it rained. He became terribly emaciated. Then one day he was gone, just as mysteriously as he had appeared.

What can you say about it? A cat, a dove, a beggar, a horse, a retarded child, the mailman. You can never really know for sure, can you? Just like you're never really sure about volcanoes. If you can, allow yourself to entertain this possibility. Believe me, you'll find yourself doing some behavior modification. And as you do it, you discover some marvelous and amazing things about your fellow creatures and about yourself. Your senses are heightened and your daily life will take on a very exciting, magical texture. Incidentally, while I was in the process of writing that you never know about volcanoes, that very week Mt. St. Helens erupted, as if to punctuate the idea. I refuse to take credit, but you must admit, it's a pretty dramatic special effect.

My dilemma in wondering how much to say about Kal was because I didn't want to butter you all over the universe. You are in the process of differentiating;

of learning what will move you forward and what will hold you back. Two very powerful symbols have been placed before you: The Living ECK Master and dirty ol' Kal Niranjan. And that's not such a hard choice, but what about all these other little things in between? The mind, the emotions, greed, anger, attachment, ego, etc., etc. What is real? What is illusion? Would you be utterly annoyed with me if I told you to relax, that gradually it will all fall into place?

I'm aware of the fact that you need to discriminate, to categorize and differentiate. Watch your fellow man, your fellow students, your teachers and leaders. At times you will see them making a mistake, or at least what appears to be a mistake. Can you accept the fact that anyone can make a mistake and that the best thing you can do with it is figure out how you can avoid doing the same thing? One mistake is to make a value judgment about the individual on the basis of his mistake. A worse thing would be to talk about it to everyone you meet. Now you are karmically entwined. Better, you use what you see and know as your own personal growth experience. We *can* grow this way. It's the most painless way of all. It's my favorite way.

So what does the advanced student see, when those who are getting started are seeing the clever, crafty hand of Kal Niranjan? They see karmic patterns being worked out, new ones forming. They see things called "set ups" and "put offs." They see the process of the test. When an individual falls into a state of negativity, they see Kal all right—but nothing more than the unleashed power of an individual's own aberrations having their day with him. In spite of our learned habits of externalizing, the "bad" things we observe in others, exist also in us. We like to think of people like Hitler, Charles Manson, Jim Jones, the murderers and charlatans who parade across the stage of history, as freaks who exist, somehow, outside of our world. They're not really human beings like the rest of us. I believe those seeds exist in all of us. Most of us simply have the controls and experiential patterns that keep such things in check. The greatest illusion about somehow separating these bad guys out of the human condition, about the possibility that they are, after all, not like us, is that we also naturally separate out and externalize the spiritual giants, the gifted, great individuals, the saviours, saints, and savants, so that it seems they, too, are some kind of freak, mutant whose glories we can never aspire to, because they are really not like us.

All of that is illusion. We have within us the potential to be unthinkably God-like, or just awfully terrible. It's really timing, evolution and carefully made choices that determine the direction any of us take. That...and free will. Although I've sometimes suspected that free will is the last illusion we overcome.

But these are great and important things we are discussing. And I'm feeling neither great nor important. Such things are better left to the big guys. But just between you and me, I find small, simple things work the most profoundly. In particular, about your thoughts, words and deeds, Paul laid out a small, easy checklist for us to use as our guide. It's so simple a lot of people ignore it, but if you take it to heart, you can ignore everything else that's been said about it. If you're not certain about a thing you're about to say or do, pose these questions to it: Is it kind? Is it true? Is it necessary? If the answer is no to any one of them, pass. Or regroup until you can say, "Yes, yes, yes." Darwin taught me another helpful and simple thing for behavior modification. He said, "Never, ever, say you're sorry." If, in your dealings with others, you are not allowed to say you're sorry in order to set things right, then you must think up what you can say and do as an alternative. It's an excellent exercise in understanding the meaning of responsibility, and so many other things that you'll simply have to try it to see what I mean.

We do need to learn to identify the things that will move us on and the things that hold us back. We need to become aware of vibratory rates. What we don't need is a Kal who is a satanic, evil, bad, malicious counter-god or devil. Kal is okay. He's got a job to do and he does it perfectly. He keeps this schoolhouse running down here. Without him there would be no school. Don't be so mean to him. When you get his number, he turns out to be a no thing. His real name is illusion.

I know only two tunes: One of them is "Yankee Doodle," and the other isn't.

—Ulysses S. Grant
1822-1885

7 The Music: The Beat of Your Own Drum

This question you've asked about feeling somewhat estranged and alienated is really important. Sometimes, when people (not me) first come into contact with these teachings they are so on fire, so exuberant and enthusiastic about what they have discovered that they cannot wait a minute to tell every single person they know all about it. Many times the person or persons they want to share with are people who have long walked congruent avenues of investigation with them; people they've spent a lot of time with in mutual growth.

It often comes as a sudden and very confusing shock when you have dumped this bag of precious gold coins all over your fellow traveler and he/she looks at you and says something like, "So??" No lights. No bingo. No jackpot. No revelation. Sometimes they go along with you for a little look and then quietly and without comment fade away...out of your orbit.

One Higher Initiate was talking about this at a major seminar. He said, "I just couldn't wait to lay all this on my friends...I mean my ex-friends."

It took me a couple of years to get enthusiastic enough to talk about it to the people who'd shared my spiritual journey up to that point.

Once I looked over my crossroads, as I asked you to do, I saw that everything we (my fellow seekers and I) had been learning was leading us ever onward to this place. Wrong: It was leading *me* to this place. Somewhere along there my road took a cut off their road. These people loved and respected me. They graciously took and read the books I proffered. One of them, a very psychically gifted woman, had a long inner visit with Paul's sister Katie. She didn't even know, up to that time, that Paul had a sister, or that she had translated from this plane. Did she later become an ECKist? Wouldn't it figure? Wrong again! She long ago joined a group of born again charismatic Christians. She is still one of my best friends. We love one another dearly. Our friendship has lasted fifteen years. But that is because we remain focused on the love we have for each other and we are willing to accept the fact that spiritually we are traveling our own individual paths. We don't try to change each other.

Sometimes I think about her and just can't figure it out. She has seen auras around people since she was a very small child. She didn't know for a long time others didn't see what she did and she would refer to people as "that blue man" or "that yellow woman." She's had clairvoyant dreams since she was young. She talks with folks who've gone over to the other side. She can hold an object in her hands and tell you its story. We used to practice "mind travel" with each other. So how come she's not beside me in this journey? I don't know. She's who and where she is and that's just right...for her.

There were a lot of people in my life prior to my stepping on this path. I was involved with many of them spiritually. Not one, family, friends, or spiritual companions, have made this step on the outer. Each one has been exposed though. It's a train I had to catch and they didn't.

Sometimes you feel lonely. Especially if you were used to sharing growth. It's even tougher if your partner or mate refuses to go along with you. Your desire to convince them springs less from a need to change who they are, than it does from a fear that you may grow very far apart. I felt that about myself and my husband. He had the same fear. The problem was, when I thought about turning back, I knew it would not save what we had between us. I saw that if I was forced to abandon my journey for the sake of his comfort, it would be disaster for both of us.

I went on with it. I simply had no choice. The drum was beating and I had to march to its beat; it was *my* beat. Somewhere along the way, Paul Twitchell cut me out of the pack and began to pour the steam to me. There was an amazing series of events that led up to that, and maybe someday I'll tell you all about it, but for now will condense it into worldly jargon. His health was frail, he had a lot to do, and very little time left to do it in. The most important thing he felt he had to do was the books he was writing. He had three different books going on three different typewriters at all times. But a lot of his time was being taken up with the monthly and quarterly publications he was doing for the chelas. He needed someone who could work closely with him, understand what he wanted done, and take the burden from him, releasing him to have more time for his writing.

Apparently he looked the situation over and decided I was the proper fodder for this assignment. I began to get calls and letters and an occasional invitation down to his office in San Diego. I know now that I did, indeed, have the potential to do these things, and a lot more. But looking back, it was another of his daily miracles that he saw it, because I was surely a diamond in the rough. He really had to clean me up and work me over before he could even stand to have me around him for any length of time. At first he did it all by long distance and all my assignments were handled through intermediaries and letters and phone calls. Looking back, it's so embarrassing all I can do is laugh. The discipline was incredible. Some of the gaffes I made are too painful to think about, even to this day. But gradually I shaped up enough for him to be able to stand being around me. Then came the next phase of my training. I had to get my vibrations to the place where I could stand being around *him*.

He did this by only working with me for a short period, and gradually increasing the length of time we spent together. In the beginning his power flows and vibrations would get to me in half an hour. Suddenly I would have such a whacking, gigantic headache that it was impossible to even think or talk. That would conclude the meeting.

Slowly, but surely, my stamina increased, my bodies made the necessary adjustments, and it got to the place where I could spend a whole day with him without flying apart at the seams.

More and more he began to trust me with assignments. Often this involved making trips for him. And closer and closer he pushed my marriage to the brink. Sometimes I had the feeling he knew it and was purposely doing it. My husband didn't understand anything about this Eckankar or about this strange man who was calling the house, filling the mailbox with letters, and sending his wife off in airplanes all over the country while he stayed home alone and wrestled with four growing kids.

I knew he was being pushed dangerously close to the edge and I also knew I was being tested severely. I was between a rock and a hard place. When things had about reached their nadir and were about to snap, Paul asked me to take one more trip. I said yes, but inside was screaming, "Why are you doing this to me? You want me to be willing to give it all up, don't you? Well...you've got your wish. This is the last straw. He'll never go for this one."

I told my husband. I was right. That was it. He started throwing things into his suitcase. He left the house with the door slamming loudly.

I stood there with tears in my eyes, wringing my hands and looking wildly around the room, crying to myself, "What shall I do? What shall I do?" My marriage and my beloved husband were terribly important to me. But my spiritual journey was everything. And so I said to Paul in my head, "Well, you've finally done it. It's a hell of a price you've made me pay."

I tried and tried to think of a way to make it all come out all right; of something to say or do to get my husband to come back home, or to get Paul to back off, but my brain was a monkey in a cage. It just ran in circles and went nowhere. Finally, there was nothing for it but to follow a principle I'd been taught. Oh what a toughy. Let go. Turn it over. I stood there and wrapped it all up and handed it to the Mahanta. I said, "*You* take care of it. However it turns out, that is the way it must be."

Suddenly I relaxed. It was all going to be all right, however it came out. How could I lose if the Mahanta was looking after it?

An hour later the front door opened and my husband walked in, dragging his suitcase, a sheepish grin on his face. "I just couldn't do it," was all he said. We hugged each other tightly. Both of us were crying. I went on the trip.

A note here about Pete, my late husband. Pete translated (died) as the first edition of this book was on the presses. He was a beautiful Soul and he gave a lot of his time, money and his wife to help Eckankar. He had many friends among the chelas. Over the years I heard him tell one or another, "I never knew Paul, and I can't explain it, but I loved him." He never read an ECK book but he had it. I was alone with him the night he translated and I very clearly saw him in his Soul body walk away with Paulji. Even in my sadness I had to smile a little knowing that at last the two friends had finally met.

I was going to give you a few tips on

this thing called "letting go" or "turning it over." But I've got a hunch you got it, through the story just told. It's not easy at first. And some things are so upsetting that the mind and emotions keep coming back into it again and again. There's been a few things I have had to let go of and turn over every five minutes for a period of hours until it stayed turned over. As with everything else, it gets easier as you work with it. The biggest problem that arises, for some, is they go off the deep end on that, once they get the hang of it. They turn over life itself and lay back and wait for the Mahanta to put their whole life together for them and make everything happen with no help from them. This never works. You can turn it over, but then you must be ready to *move*. Trust that your actions are guided, but in many cases you will be called upon for action. Sometimes it's totally out of your hands as in the life or death situation of a loved one. If you do this exercise you will be amazed at the inner peace and acceptance you can come into in such crisis. I have many times seen this one principle turn a horrifying, heart-wrenching, unbearable situation into an experience of incredible beauty. I've seen people use it, and turn what could have been the worst experience of their lives into one of the finest. But if you need a job and you turn it over, don't lie back on your bed and wait for General Motors to call and offer you the presidency. It's not likely to happen. Even for the Mahanta to get you a job you've got to get out there and find the people who are going to give it to you.

As you enter more seriously into this role called chela (by the way, that's pronounced cheela), you may run into some resistance from others in your life. Here's a handy phrase to remember if that should come up. *"The people in your life have a vested interest in you remaining as you are."* It helps a lot if you can be loving, diplomatic, and understanding. They don't know what it is you're doing and they're afraid. A few years down the trail they'll find you just as wonderful and special as you are now, actually—even more so, and they'll be more relaxed. In fact they may begin to ask you some questions once they see you haven't fallen off the edge of the world.

A few who have embarked on this journey have had relatives who had no idea what Eckankar was about, raise a really heavy ruckus. One couple who mistook ECK for a cult had their ECKist son kidnapped and deprogrammed. The problem was, there was nothing to deprogram. All he had was the awareness of his own unique self that he'd grown into. The programmer learned in that experience: You can only deprogram a mind that's been programmed and tampered with. You can make a mind rethink. But there is no way a Soul can unknow. If that family had taken the time to find out what Eckankar is really about, they'd have avoided that expensive and traumatic mistake. As it is, they're awfully lucky if they haven't become an *ex*-family.

The difference from a person and an angel is easy. Most of an angel is in the inside and most of a person is on the outside.

—Fynn
Mister God, This is Anna

8 <u>Program Notes</u>

Right after our first awareness of one another, I found myself jotting down notes. As we've gone along a lot of those notes fell into the different subjects we've gone over. Only looking at them now, do I realize that we've been wandering over some pretty complex trails. From what some of you "beginners" have been pulling out of me, I'd say you began a very long time ago.

One of my notes says, "Create!" It's hard to believe we've come this far without that coming up.

Among the ECKists you'll find many gifted, creative, innovative individuals. They didn't all come in that way. I've seen literally hundreds, who as they unfolded into their own unknown, untested areas found music there, found poetry, prose, art. I had never published one piece of writing prior to my studying ECK. And at the ripe old age of forty I suddenly bought and began playing a piano, though I'd never studied music before in this life.

Musicians who've studied for years take

up new instruments, begin composing original pieces. They use their inner faculties to enhance a subject they've long ago mastered.

This is really exciting. We just have no idea of the wonderful and different things that are in us to do until we begin to open ourselves to them. You'll read a lot in the publications about getting out the message of ECK. It sounds like we're proselytizing all over the place. But just as with most of the things we've gone over, it is not at all what it seems. Nobody needs to sell ECK. At our seminars you won't see people being whipped into an emotional, revivalist frenzy. Or as some of the cults and religions do, giving you a hot bath in our overwhelming love for you.

What you see at an ECK Seminar or a Day of ECK or an Introductory Lecture are a lot of Souls expressing themselves creatively. In a sense they are not doing all this for you, they are doing it because it's a marvelous experience for them. Creativity is the most joyous work of Soul. As Soul becomes ever more the guiding force in our lives, It begins to express Its nature or It begins to desire that. You can hold it off, saying, "I can't write music," or whatever. But that's not *you* saying that. It's you know what. And it's not a fatal attack, just a small fainting spell. In this one thing I am confident: A few years of study under your belt and you'll never recognize yourself in the terms of what you have explored and accomplished creatively. And we have a lot of outer activities going on because we are creative, happy entities channeling and flowing from the inner to the outer. We're who we are when we are doing this. If you never feel like doing it, that's okay. But if you later decide you'd like to try the experience, there's a way and a place for it to happen. You can bring some of the beauty within to the outside, and let that say to others what it will. When someone later comes up to you and says, "You touched something very deep within me," you'll be so glad you had the experience. That is what it means, spreading the message of ECK. It's done in a million ways. Somewhere, somehow, someone touched you. Or you wouldn't be here. It was a happy thing for both of you.

But the message "Create!" goes deeper. In the very beginning, when the inner life is starting to become energized, unless you already have creative outlets, a lot of what is going on beneath the surface isn't seen.

You dream but you don't remember. You contemplate but you can't make anything out of what's happening there. And the mind either tries to tear it apart or put labels on it that don't really relate.

The texture of the inner life and experience is often just too fine and subtle for us to accept what goes on there as real at first. The mind throws up buzz words that are intended as put downs: Imagination, fantasy, daydreams, etc. But there's the rub. Those categories are the texture of the inner experience.

Poetry is the *texture* too. And it is very often the bridge between the two worlds. It is far easier to bring out the inner experience in poetry...it flows that way. Music and art are the same. They are ways to use physical symbols to express the inner texture. Using words, the thing I'm doing now, the thing Paul Twitchell did so powerfully, is the most difficult of all ways to translate the inner to the outer. If you are already involved in some form of artistic expression, use your art to express what is in there and difficult to describe. Even if you've never tried it, get some paints and do whatever comes. Or sit and write a poem about it, or a song. If it has to be prose, try fiction. Have you never done such a thing? It's the best reason I know for doing it now. You don't have to show it to anybody, you know. Don't do it for show and tell. Do it for you. Just make it be, as close as you can, what it's like right now in your inner worlds. Don't mentalize it... play at it freely as a child would do. Children. How very close they are to it. Another note says "Lessons."

Lessons

Experiences are the threads that we weave into our life tapestry. Without them we have no life to speak of. The more awareness we have, the more we understand that each and every experience we have has a reason...maybe many reasons. We ECKists are incessantly turning our experiences over and looking inside and underneath and all about them. We are constantly asking ourselves, "Why am I doing this?" "What is the reason for this?" "What is *really* going on here?" We know that our experiences usually have much deeper meanings for us than the surface. We know that things are seldom what they seem. We know that if we go through a heavy or uncomfortable experience and we don't see why—we don't get the lesson of it—it's a good chance we'll have to do it again. We have all heard people say that a certain thing has happened repeatedly to them and they wonder why it has to be them it always happens to. We've all got something of that sort in our personal history. It happens to us repeatedly because there's something in there we need to learn about. It's not a constant, but more times than not when we finally see what it is for, it doesn't happen anymore.

It's not always easy to see what a certain experience is about while we're in the middle of it. But when it's over, or the intense part of it has leveled out, it often becomes apparent. This becomes ever more so as Soul gets in control, for we are often led to do or say a certain thing, call a certain person, go to a certain place and we don't know why. It's just a feeling, a hunch, an intuition, an inexplicable desire (all of those things are also the texture of the inner experience) that we don't understand but feel we have to do. These are my favorite things. Be alert, there's big magic afoot.

After we've followed the inner impulse, something will take place. It may be a brief encounter or a long drawn out series of happenings, but when it's run its course, you say, "Ah...now I know why I did that." Sometimes when doing a talk, I have suddenly found myself wandering off on some side road, talking about something that has nothing to do with the subject at hand. All of a sudden it will wind down, and there I am stuck off to the side with nowhere else to go with it, no apparent point to it, and no logical way to tie it to my main theme. For a moment it's unnerving. But you carry on. I've learned to just share with the audience what's happened. I usually say, "Well...I don't know what that was all about, maybe somebody here does," because I learned from long experience that when that has happened and puzzled me, sure enough afterwards someone will come up and shake my hand and tell me that that thing I said, the side trip, was the one thing they most needed to hear and gain some insight about. They are so appreciative, so deeply grateful, that it's almost embarrassing. And I am equally appreciative and grateful to them for sharing it with me, because they show me the ECK was working. They reinforce my willingness to be a channel, in spite of the fact that I know I must be looking a little silly at times. And speaking of silly, that brings me to my next note: "Laugh!"

A Sense of Humor

One of the greatest gifts I've ever received was on my birthday in 1973. Some dear friends gave me a copy of *The Little Prince*. There is a part of me that is him. I am not always the Little Prince. Sometimes I think and act like a grownup and get very carried away with "matters of importance." But it usually doesn't last too long. The Little Prince in me is a very significant person in my personal universe, and no matter how weighty the matters are I'm allowing to occupy my attention, the Little Prince is very near the surface and is bound to pop off before long.

I find I am only willing to take the matters of this world seriously to a certain point...and in small doses. There's work to do, for sure, like sweeping out your volcano every day, and watering your flower, and pulling up the weeds. Those are just things that have to be done to keep your world in shape. But so many of the things we worry about are a waste of time and energy.

I remember once worrying for a whole solid week about Southern California breaking off and dropping into the sea. It colored everything in my life a dark, bilious brown. And what good did it do me? Or Southern California? None that I've ever been able to see. I finally got sick of worrying about it and stopped. California remained above sea level. I hadn't been holding it off with all that worrying, that was obvious. I haven't remembered to worry about it for a long time, and it's still here. As much as I hate to say it, the matter didn't need me.

Years ago, before becoming a chela in ECK, I used to worry about everything. I would start off in the morning with how clean I was getting my teeth, the kid's, the bills, and the dog's fleas. By the time the day was half over I'd gotten to the economy, the crooked politicians, the situation with the Russians, the Gnomes of Zurich, and the Pope's health. There was simply no end to the things that needed to be worried about. And once I had covered the world, I couldn't relax. What kind of a woman would my oldest son marry? He was already eight years old. You have to keep on top of these things. If night hadn't fallen yet, and I ran out of things, I could always worry about what kind of world this would be for my unborn grandchildren.

I haven't thought for a long time about that old self. The Little Prince in me has the upper hand and he says, "Let the grownups worry about all those 'matters of importance,' it's time to watch a sunset."

Once I began to see what this is all about down here, I found myself laughing. More and more, it seems to be a riddle, a giant cosmic joke. One by one the illusions are dropping away and as each one falls away from us, we turn around and look at it and we have to laugh. Death? Once so scary, once so ominous and frightening we could barely speak the word, let alone really think about it. I can laugh about it. Not the experience, but at my old thought forms. Why? Because there is no such thing.

As the veils of illusion slip away, there is less and less to worry about and we really begin to know what it means to be free; free to watch a beautiful sunset, free to laugh.

The Little Prince in me really came into its own during the time I worked side-by-side with Paul Twitchell. Once I got over being scared to death of him, and got my bodies' vibrations adjusted to being around him, we entered into a friendship of sorts. The role of pupil and teacher, the awareness of what was really going on was always there, and certain lines were never crossed. But these things became realities that just "were" without being overwhelming, and one of the reasons it was possible was Paul's gentle, sensitive ways and his incredible sense of humor.

Paul, once he trusted you and felt relaxed with you, was one of the most humorous people I have ever known. He had an almost childlike love of a good joke, a funny story, a clever punch line. I think it was his release valve from all the matters of importance he was working with. Often he used his sense of humor to keep me at ease with him. Certainly he provided me with many valuable lessons in teaching through humor.

Once I sent him a long letter. In it were the details of the business I was doing for him. Also included were ideas for some future work, a review of a seminar, what my Satsang Class was doing, the weather report and, probably, what I had for dinner last night. It was terribly thoughtless of me. The man was trying to finish up *The Shariyat-Ki-Sugmad*, Book Two before his body gave out. These are the kind of disparities in realities that boggle the mind. Paul had something he had to get over to me. He would never say, "Remember who I am and who you are." He would never say, "I have terribly important matters on my mind and you're wasting my time." He wasn't like that anyway, and he knew a direct reprimand would simply crush me into non-functioning. He knew my mistake was innocent and friendly. But it was thoughtless. He taught me with gentle humor. Here's what he did.

He had this teddy bear in which he had imbued all the qualities and the personality of the Little Prince. When I would arrive, the teddy bear would be in different set ups. Sometimes he was out in the yard watching the birds and keeping the rabbits out of the garden. Sometimes he was watching television. Bear, which was his name, was a force in that household and he was always in the middle of things.

The day I arrived following his receipt of my long, newsy letter, it was obvious I'd been set up. The table where we always worked was filled, as usual, with Paul's papers. But right in the middle of the table, spread out, was my long letter. Bear was sitting on top of it, wearing Paul's glasses and bent over it, as if he were reading.

Paul was laughing softly. "Well, Patti," he said, "Your letter was just too long for me, I had to put Bear to work on it. He's going to give me the condensed version." I couldn't help laughing. Just about that time Bear fell over. He went into a dead faint. Paul and Gail and I were laughing then. I picked Bear up, remeoved Paul's glasses from his face and petted his head. I said, "Sorry, Bear, I didn't mean to put you to all that strain. Next time I'll make it short and stick to the point and you won't have to work so hard." And you can believe that I did. After that, all letters were brief, to the point, and major points numbered and underlined. He didn't have to give me a whack with the Rod of Power. It was accomplished perfectly by hitting me over the head with a soft, funny, little teddy bear, thus allowing me to live to tell about it. I daresay the Living ECK Master has had occasion to be grateful, at times, for what Bear taught me.

I am often invited to attend seminars around the country to be a guest speaker.

If it were possible, I'd go to every one of them, but unfortunately I have to turn down most because of my schedule. There was a certain month that I had vowed to keep free to catch up on my writing and had done it too, then one day I got a letter from a fellow initiate I had met briefly in Baltimore. This was a sales pitch for me to attend a seminar in the forbidden month. It was truly the funniest letter I ever remember receiving. I was in my office reading it and my husband heard me laughing clear down at the other end of the house. I laughed for days over that letter and finally said to myself, "Well, I guess I could make *one* trip that month." Anyone who can make me laugh that hard is someone I've got to know better.

When I was the editor of the *ECK World News*, I put a cuckoo clock on the wall right behind my desk. Everytime I'd get to expounding on something and feel I was working on very important matters, it seemed that little bird would come out and yell, "Cuckoo, cuckoo, cuckoo!" His timing was uncanny. We all laughed. It's very humbling, difficult to get to feeling you're terribly important when you're subjected to those kinds of editorial comments.

A lot of the situations we get ourselves into are not funny at all. But once we're out of it we look back and we can see that the thing was, in effect, a parable. Or, we can find a humorous, or light parable that applies and it's a marvelous mechanism for lifting our spirits and the heaviness of what is happening.

One of my favorite parables I have often told in my talks is the story of the little fellow who was an incurable optimist, whose parents, hoping to balance him out into a more realistic approach to life, locked him for several days in a room full of horse manure. He had no toys, books, T.V., or other goodies. At the end of the exile they opened the door and found him as sunny and happy and smiling as ever. He barely looked up at them as he was gleefully digging around in the manure.

"What in the world are you doing?" his parents cried out. The little optimist looked up smiling. "I'm digging," he said, "I've been digging ever since you put me in here. I just know with all this manure around there's a pony in here somewhere!"

It's happened more than once that life has become a series of problems for me or one of my friends, and just when we think it can't get worse, it does. Right in the middle of a recitation of woes, one of us will pop it out: "There's a pony in here somewhere."

Another of my favorite parables is one that has seen me through a lot of situations where my best laid plans all fall apart, or a friend has seen a cherished dream smashed beyond recall. It is an experience that once happened to my late husband's uncle. This one works in many ways and contains many messages.

Uncle Bill was born and raised in a silver mining town high in the mountains of New Mexico. Life was hard for the miners and their families, and daily existence was a struggle. Money was scarce and luxuries were unknown. But Bill was a dreamer and he was always looking for a way to get rich.

He left the mountains and tried his hand at many different things, but his real goal was to get as rich as he could, as fast as he could, with as little work as he could.

The day finally came and he smelled the answer to his dreams when he met up with a man who raised silver foxes for the furriers. All Bill had to do was invest his life savings in a male and female silver fox, and sit back and let nature take its course. He was assured that the one abiding interest of silver foxes was to make as many new little silver foxes as fast as they can.

Bill gave the man his life's savings and one day he pulled his old beat up car into the mining town with the caged pair of young foxes securely tied to the roof. The little town was abuzz at the prospect of having its first millionaire.

As Bill explained it, because of the nature of the foxes, the male and female were kept in separate cages until it was time to mate them. Carefully he constructed his separate kennels, and in between them he built an "L" shaped runway with gates at both ends.

Some time went by while he awaited the maturing of the foxes. And finally the big day came. The male was frantically trying to get out of his cage and visit the lady who was so tantalizingly near, yet so far. Bill's excitement was great. All he had to do now to become a millionaire was open the two doors of the runway and let mother nature do the rest.

When he opened the door of the male's cage, the fox shot out of there like a racehorse. Bill figured he must have been going about sixty miles an hour when he hit the "L" in the runway, broke his neck and died on the spot.

Bill never did become a millionaire. But he was the best story teller I ever met and he had a gift for laughing at himself and at life that made everybody love him and want to be around him. He could always be prevailed upon to tell any gathering about his silver fox escapade and he always ended it by saying, "One minute I was about to be a millionaire and fifteen seconds later I was out of business." In spite of it (or maybe because of it) Bill was one of the richest men I ever knew.

One of my favorite funny stories from the days of the *ECK World News* involves the famous "Swiss Consultant," a tiny, fuzzy toy owl that came to oversee our creative endeavors.

When the "consultant" arrived, his stated purpose was to "keep things in order" around there. We sat him on top of my cuckoo clock. Keeping order was evidently not at all what he was about. I've never really understood it, but as soon as we put the owl on the clock, Woodstock, the little yellow bird who lived in there, went berserk. Up until that time, Woodstock had only come out on the hour and the half hour. Once that Swiss Consultant perched on the clock, he began coming out and yelling "cuckoo" whenever he felt like it. There was no rhyme or reason to his appearances. He might miss the hour by ten minutes and then go off three times in a row at five-minute intervals. The amount of "cuckoos" ceased to have any connection with what time it was.

Things didn't settle down until we decided the whole thing was a territorial matter and moved the Swiss over across the room to the file cabinet. Woodstock went back to his normal routine—mostly. He never completely recovered.

Machines responded to this kind of wonder and humor also. Every so often Paul would get mischievous in the casinos in Las Vegas. The machines there seemed to love him. Often, when he and Gail needed change for the laundromat, Paul would supply it by stopping by a slot machine, which was only too happy to oblige him. The slot machines in Vegas were so happy to see Paul that in several casinos he was asked not to come back.

Elevators were also friends. At one seminar, a bunch of us were waiting for what seemed an extraordinarily slow elevator system. Paul was standing there too. It must have been easily seven or eight minutes before one finally came. People began to push into the long awaited car, while Paul lagged behind. When we were all jammed in, we called and beckoned to Paul to join us. He said quietly, "No, I'll take another one." This seemed an odd decision since the system was so sluggish. But, at that exact instant a door behind him opened, and the twenty or so of us gaped as the doors closed on him in his own private car.

I am aware that some of my readers will wonder if I am not making up these seemingly real events that transpired around stuffed animals and machines. I assure you, they happened, just as I report them. What I have done in telling them is to take you into the magic world of possibilities. In this world, we are functioning in the mode called "be as a little child." The supposedly inanimate and the mechanical objects around us, as well as the animal world, patterned themselves around our senses of wonder and fun; and because we agreed that these things could be, they were. In a sense, we created them, but in another, mysterious sense, the creations then began to play with us and create fun for us.

I could write a whole new book just on the subject of using our imaginative faculties to create the world around us that we need and want. Suffice it to say, all of us needed a world of gentle fun and laughter and the world around us responded to that necessity.

Harold, the present Mahanta, the Living ECK Master, has an utterly delightful sense of humor. His is very dry and subtle. When he is speaking at an Eckankar seminar the room frequently reverberates with laughter. At one seminar he told the story of how his wife, Marjorie, was so often on the phone working on her projects that it was sometimes difficult to have a word with her. One evening, needing her attention, he took a dime from the dresser, drove down to a pay phone, called her up and asked to have a few words with her.

In the process of a new writing project, I have spent many hours in Harold's study taping interviews with him. He's a fascinating raconteur and most of his tales have an amusing point to them or if the point is very serious, somehow he finds ways to laugh at himself and the human condition along the way. Harold's subtle sense of humor shines like a beacon through the anecdotes in his book, *The Wind of Change*.

I'm very fond of quoting good ideas, wherever I find them, so I'll leave you with this one which pretty much covers it:

A good sense of humor is a blend of wit and wisdom.

—Chinese Fortune Cookie
1983

I knew a man, and whether he was
in the body or out of it I cannot
say, but he was caught up to the
third heaven, Caught into Paradise
and heard unspeakable words which
it is not lawful for man to utter.
                    —2 Corinthians 12

9 The Leading Man

You've been asking about the Master for a long time and I've been holding you off. I've felt your restlessness and urgency almost daily. It hasn't been because it's not that important, but because it's the best part. Up until now we've been working on the appetizers. This is the main course.

It's so special and dear to me that I had to hold off until we became better acquainted and I felt completely comfortable in sharing the most important thing in my existence with you.

I've already told about the testy proposition I made to Paul Twitchell the first time I wrote to him. I said I'd keep an open mind, but he'd have to prove the things he said before I'd believe them. When I think back to the strange inner experiences that led to my buying that first book, it's a wonder that didn't convince me all by itself. But the fact was, it didn't. Neither, really, did my first exposure to Paul at the meeting. I just went along, doing my life, reading the discourses, and allowing Paul Twitchell and Eckankar a tiny compartment in my universe. If I had any master at all that I was aware of, it was Jesus. I was disillusioned with the church, but very attached to him.

Shortly after I first saw Paul in Los Angeles my life took an unexpected turn. We had built a large addition on our house to accommodate four growing kids. We were aware when we did it we had overbuilt for the neighborhood and were buried in terms of selling it and getting our investment out. In those days California real estate had not reached the state of frenzy it has now. That was to come years in the future. We decided to build the addition with the understanding that the space was important to our sanity and we'd commit ourselves to staying there ten more years. We'd lived with the new addition two or three years when I began studying Eckankar. About the time of the Los Angeles meeting, life in the area we lived began to get uncomfortable. Drugs were becoming a problem. Youth gangs were prowling. Flashers were accosting the little kids on their way home from school. But we were coping. Then one night at dinner my husband blurted out unexpectedly, "How would you like to move?" I'd never allowed myself to entertain the thought. "Where?" I asked in surprise. "Down to the beach where we've been vacationing."

I couldn't believe that such a wonderful thing could happen. But the next day I hit the freeway and began househunting. I felt silly doing it and was sure if I found anything we'd never be able to dump the old house. The house next door had been on the market three years.

But, as if the wheels had been pregreased, I found my dream house at the beach, we bought it, sold the other one just in time and got every dime out of it we put in. It was a miracle.

How I loved my new home. All spread out before me was a panoramic view of the sea. Windows everywhere, in contrast to the closed in, almost prisonlike, construction of the old house. I could never get enough of it. I floated through that house as if it were a magic castle.

One day, I was standing at the dining room window looking out at the sea, and looking around me at all the beauty of my surroundings feeling so grateful and blessed, when suddenly a small voice within me spoke a line that I must have read in some of the ECK writings that had held no meaning for me at the time. The voice said, "When the chela has been on the path a year, he will look around at his life and scarcely recognize it."

I started looking around me. My whole being was in a kind of suspended animation. If anybody could look around their life and scarcely recognize it, it was me. I thought carefully—counting: My twelfth discourse was that minute on the way to me in the mails. The hair raised up all over my body.

"He did it! He did it! He actually brought it off. He proved something to me. Paul Twitchell...Paul...

Suddenly my eyes filled with tears as I said the new word to myself. "Chela. I...am...a...Chela." I'm having a hard time writing this to you, my friend, because I find my eyes once again unexpectedly brimming over with tears and it's hard to see. All of a sudden that tiny compartment in my universe became my universe. Of course it had been happening all along, but I just hadn't seen it.

Following on the heels of this revelation was the immediate understanding that Paul had been there beside me all that time. He had been with me. It was then I stopped saying he, and realized I could talk to him directly.

"Master. I have a real, personal, spiritual master. *You* are my master." And then it hit me. All along—he'd been there waiting. And I'd given him nothing. Worse, I'd criticized and belittled him. And he'd been watching. Now came the guilt and remorse. I was so ashamed of my stubbornness, my lack of awareness. All this time he'd been working behind the scenes and look how I'd repaid him. My understanding that he'd delivered, as promised, created waves of love for him within me. But the knowledge of how awfully I had behaved toward him overshadowed it all and I was consumed with shame and self-reproach.

I walked weakly to the kitchen sink and held onto it to steady myself. The pain of what I was knowing was almost unbearable. How could I go on? How could I ever make it up to him?

And then something new happened. Something came over me I had never, up to that time, experienced. It started at the top of my head and ran down all over me. It felt like thick, warm syrup enveloping me. It was love, so affirming, so unconditional and complete that all thoughts of guilt and repentance dissolved in it. It was totally impossible to look back, to blame myself, to feel anything bad. I knew that not only was I forgiven, but I'd never done anything to be forgiven for. I also knew, beyond a shadow of doubt, because that was the distinct message: "Nothing matters but this moment and what you have come to in it." I had experienced what is called, "The Presence and the Love of the Master." That thing that I'd seen in Los Angeles, that encircled Paul and those ladies: Now it encircled me—and I was no longer on the outside.

I want to say right here that this was *my* experience. Yours will probably be quite different, but it will come. The greatest difficulty surrounding these kinds of discussions is people tend to accept what they hear as the norm, and if they don't have a similar experience they think they haven't got it yet. I know people who for years, thought they hadn't experienced something, who discounted what was really going on, because of some preconceived notion they had formed from the books or what others told them. That's the real difficulty in communicating the spiritual life, and if you do anything, spare yourself that setback. Have your experiences and know they are all part of it, even if you've never heard of it happening that way, or if it isn't at all what you expect and think it should be. Why wait two or three years to finally understand that you were getting it, but didn't realize it because you were expecting something else?

Some of my experiences are very dramatic, but that doesn't mean they are more spiritual than someone else's whose are more subtle and difficult to express. More than likely it means that I was so obtuse and hard-headed that I had to be clobbered with an experience before I'd know I had one. And then there's always the factor of individual uniqueness. The Masters give us exactly what we need. The Soul-self takes us the way that is best for us. The best thing I can tell you is to trust that, as a student of the ECK, you are always on sacred ground. Everything is part of it, good, bad, and indifferent, and you are very special. Therefore everything that happens to you is very special and fraught with meaning. If you don't think so, you just haven't realized it yet. But you will.

The ECK Masters tell you to love your

life and give it its fullest measure of importance. You do this by always assuming you are succeeding and making progress and you use no one else's yardstick. Everytime you compare yourself or your experience with another, you defeat yourself, whether you come up short or smelling like a rose in the comparison.

There was a time when a certain individual was constantly bombarding me with recalls of past lives we had shared together. I had absolutely no reality on this. Everytime I heard it, it was strange and unfamiliar. Not only did I not have similar recalls concerning this person, I wasn't having any about anyone.

One day I was having lunch with Paul and telling him about this. I said that this person was so far beyond me in spiritual development that I felt like I'd never get there. He listened carefully and then he laughed. He said, "Did it ever occur to you, Patti, that you may be farther ahead in your progress than this person?" I found the idea astonishing. I also understood that he wasn't saying I *was* more highly developed. He was telling me that the yardstick I was using was irrelevant.

Sometimes life at my house seems mundane, and then suddenly it picks up in energy and significance. Perhaps it's because of this book, and because the ECK Masters have a keen interest in what I'm doing, they are quite tangibly present.

Paul showed up about a week or so before the book began. I was in the process of folding a two-page letter I'd written on a particularly perplexing and vexing situation in regard to some former loving and devoted friends of his who, subsequent to his leaving, found themselves not enjoying the same highly personal attention from the Living ECK Master. Instead of being willing to take a back seat to their former prominence within Eckankar, they chose to move away and attack. Having been a very close, first-hand witness to their relationships with Paul, the things they did to help him and Eckankar, it puzzled and grieved me to see them now joining hands with forces they would formerly have detested and personally attacking the life's work of the man they loved.

I was, frankly, utterly annoyed with their perfidy; with the strange blindness that permitted them to have been able to bask in the power of one who befriended them and then, when the glory faded, to call back all they had said and done. I inveighed against the kind of tunnel vision that could allow anyone to love and support Paul Twitchell and enjoy his personal friendship and find themselves able to attack his life's work and feel they were not in any way hurting him. I had said in the letter, "To do this requires the kind of reasoning that can separate the moon from the tides. It is impossible to separate Paul Twitchell from his life's work. It was what he existed for and if you knew him at all, you knew that."

As I folded this letter, still burning and afire with my irritation and perplexity, I suddenly felt that old familiar warmth from my right ear down my back to the solar plexis; the subtle pressure of being hugged lightly. Everything inside me went on alert. Then I heard, in my right ear, the familiar chuckle, and the accent that cannot be mistaken. The first thing that was said was, "You're a hard person to get through to. Your line is busy a lot." I had to laugh. "Okay, I'm listening." What came out was a few words I was to record as dictation. I did my best, but once my mind "edited" and I wrote a word that I thought fit better and made more sense. I was sternly corrected to write it exactly as said. There weren't many words. It was short, and incredibly simple. In one small paragraph, I had before me the explanation of the dilemma I had been struggling with through 2 pages, single-line, typed. It was so simple that I marvelled that I'd not seen it. This is what Paul had to say in explaining the antagonistic behavior of his one-time friends and loyal followers:

Those who fight the ECK are drawing the same power and recognition from It as when they supported me [sic]. It's all the same thing, don't you see—for or against—they're still using my power. They use . . . they will not settle for what they'd have left without using me, whichever way it is done.

Once he was working around here and I had my frequency tuned in, I found myself doing an incredible amount of spiritual writing; the great love of *his* life. *Coincidence*, no doubt.

When this book was first shown to me, I knew I would do it. I really wanted to. But I have had other things like that, that got lost somehow in the daily shuffle. However, the morning after we met, the phone rang. It was the Master. He hadn't called me in over a year. He was just saying "Hi" and that he loved me, but I knew why. I blurted the whole thing out, what had occurred in the night about this book. "Do it!" was all he said. It was sealed. There was no way I could forget. And since this is for you, you can see that the Living ECK Master was working behind the scenes in your life in the Spring of 1980.

I am a fairly articulate communicator, but find myself stumbling a little in introducing you to the Master. It's almost sixteen years now since Paul moved into my life, and there really are no words to describe this bond or what it has meant to me. And whether Harold will be your Master or one who comes after him, you'll never find the words either. But if it is yours to experience in this lifetime, you will have one knowing: It was an appointment you made long before this present life began. That's why words are inadequate. There is so much involved, for each of us, in this meeting that we can never know it all, but we sense it.

In the beginning I was afraid to read

the book I'd come upon about Paul Twitchell. It lay on the coffee table a week. Everytime I'd pass by it, I'd experience uneasiness. I knew instinctively that he was going to ask something of me, something I would have to make a choice about. I was afraid it would change my life—and I liked my life fine, just the way it was.

When I read it and wrote to him, I was holding myself away, as I was in that first meeting. Later I was to understand that I wasn't being difficult and unaware. On the contrary, bubbling very close to the surface was a great awareness, too much. Innately I knew if I kept this appointment, it could not be a half-way thing. Beneath the surface I knew what would be asked of me; what was to come. It took me a long time, but I eventually realized I'd done all this before, and I blew it badly. Sometime I had reached the inner circle of the Master, gone through the higher initiations, and then made a gigantic error. And this is true of many of us. We just keep coming back until we get it right.

One day I was working on *The Mystic World*. The pictures and articles were all laid out before me on the table. There was a picture of Paul, smiling up at me.

Suddenly I was staring at it, and my entire being was flooded with memory. I have known him before. I was knowing it. *Where was it? What was it?* The knowledge of it hung there, right at the edge of consciousness. Any second I would have it. I pushed at it, tried to reach around that corner, but it wouldn't come. It was maddening, because the knowledge that it was there was total. I just couldn't extricate it.

Another little scene I blew occurred on the occasion of my second initiation. I had actually met Paul for the first time three months before. Now I was waiting for him in a hotel lobby. He came in, greeted me, and we walked to the elevator which would take us to his suite of rooms where the initiation would take place. As we rode up the elevator together, he seemed to get a dreamy, trance-like, far away look. (Something I would see thousands of times later.) Softly, he said, "It's been a long time, Patti. A long, long time." Existing, as I did, in my wonderful state of oblivion, I hadn't the faintest notion what he was talking about. It struck me as funny. I laughed, "It's only been three months, Paul," I corrected him. For a second he seemed confused, and then he shook his head and was back in present time. Kindly he smiled and apologized for mumbling absent-mindedly.

I knew almost immediately that he'd been seeing and referring to something else. But my lack of awareness had shut him off. This was my first lesson from the physical Master. I never got a second chance on that. I was never allowed to ask or to know. To this day I do not know, consciously. But I know I could have had it, if I hadn't stupidly shot off my mouth in that elevator. It took a few more lessons of that sort, of me closing doors that were never again allowed to open, before I learned to listen and stay in neutral when something important was quietly run by me.

It takes tremendous sensitivity and stamina to work with one of these Masters on a personal basis. You can never allow yourself to become fully relaxed, because the minute you let your guard down, you find yourself with your foot in your mouth. Once a dear friend of mine who was on a very chummy basis with Paul, called him and was chatting. In the course of the conversation she began grumbling about someone. Suddenly, Paul, who was usually very soft spoken, turned hard.

"Don't ever complain to me about an ECKist!" he said sharply and slammed down the phone, hanging up on her. She was a very close and personal friend of his. But she was also a chela and she'd wandered, unthinkingly, across that invisible boundary. It's surprisingly easy to do because of the great love the Master has for us, and because they give us space. At times things can get so friendly and relaxed that one can be lulled into forgetting the invisible line. By the time I'd worked with Paul Twitchell a year and a half, I'd seen so many ways the Higher Initiate can blow it that it was little wonder this was not my first trip.

This working closely with the physical Master is not a task everyone will do. If it is to be your lot, you are in for some tough testing, and it is an experience unlike any other you've had on the planet. No matter how bright, how wonderful and successful you've been in any other field or business, here the standard rules of success don't apply. The rules are all different. And they have a way of shifting and rearranging themselves on an almost daily basis.

The people who have the toughest time in Eckankar are those who are brilliant at learning the rules of any game and feel once they've got it down pat, they've mastered it. Inevitably when the rules change, they will insist on sticking to the old ones thinking they are right, because that's how it was (or they thought it was) when they learned it. Unless this kind of individual is willing, immediately, to suspend this kind of fixed, rigid approach, he or she will zoom into and out of the Master's physical orbit at something approaching the speed of sound. Having watched it a lot, I came to the idea that it was most often a set up. The heady wine of instant access to the power centers, rapidly followed by an eviction into the boondocks. The ones who have the most difficulty are those who insist on believing the ECK and the Master will follow predictable patterns. I have found only one rule in all this that has remained constant: Change.

Many people who have undergone such experiences were too hung up on the Outer Master. They put so much attention there that they failed to establish an awareness and a communication system with the Inner Master. One who does this misses the point in ECKANKAR. I was going to say 98% and the Master just corrected me—99% of the work that the

Living ECK Master of the time is performing is behind the scenes on the inner planes. So this physical vehicle that we see, and hear, and sometimes work with is but a pin dot shadow of his reality. Think of it: When he speaks or writes in the physical world you are getting one percent of what is available to you, what he has waiting for you when you meet and use him in your inner life.

There is another factor to the Master that is important to understand. Some people, who have a good and constant inner dialogue and connection with the Master think that the physical Master carries around in his head a full awareness of everything that passes between them on the inner. This is another confusion about the Inner and Outer Master. Regardless of the immense reality and powers of the Living ECK Master, the physical vehicle is a human being, just as you and I. Could your mind carry the details of 99% of the inner and outer lives of hundreds of thousands of people simultaneously?

Harold Klemp, the human being, does not consciously think about you and everything you are doing every day. He doesn't have to. But if it is necessary, he can concentrate and know. When he meets you or reads a letter from you, he tunes in on the 99% and he knows all about you. In those moments the outer and the inner join. His spiritual self is always with you, working, testing, guiding and most of all loving you. There in that dimension he exists and functions for you alone. And this he can do simultaneously with every single Chela. How? Time and Space are not involved in the matter. This is the exclusive domain of the Divine ECK, Itself, and in that all things are possible.

It is very special, to be able to see and hear the Living ECK Master. The inner life becomes highly energized from the experience. As I told my little friend, "Feast your eyes, that is what he's here for." But you'd better believe that is not all that he's doing. Perhaps what's been said here will enable you to get a clearer picture. But as it is with something like this, I am painfully aware of the inadequacy of my words. They, too, can be no more than one percent of what is.

I am aware that my experience in working under the direct personal supervision of three Masters is an uncommon one. But most of the things I relate are analogous to every chela's spiritual journey with the Masters. More than once, as Paul was talking to me, teaching me, sharing his life history and his visions, I would ask myself, "Why is he giving me all this? Why is he spending so much of his physical time and attention on me?" Sure, he needed me to help free up his time to get his books written. But that was too obvious. And there was too much more going on for it to be only that. I lived with the constant awareness that what was going on between us was not exactly what it seemed to be. But what it was, I never really figured out, until this moment. It all happened like that, because I would, in the future, share it with you. The Masters have their things to say to you, and that is the big stuff, the overview. But what I have to say is also important, because I am one of you. I am a reporter, who chronicles this unique and incredible journey from your side of that invisible line. And doesn't it figure that the task would fall to the Doubting Thomas, the stubborn hardhead who refused to believe anything she hadn't first proved by experience? Who had to get hit over the head with an experience before she'd accept the fact that she'd had one?

Well—a lot of information gatherers

are gone now. A lot of people who figured the outer works and the outer Master were all that this path was about are gone now. A lot of people who sought to use the path and the Living ECK Master for their own egos and personal power, were themselves used briefly, and they are gone now. And here's one who wanted no part of it, who tried to run away, but had to follow the beat of her own drum. And I'm still here. There is no place for me to go. For what all this is, I am. And wherever I go, I take it with me. There are many like me. You'll meet them as you journey along.

There are those for whom Eckankar is a brief encounter, a momentary opening which is only for that purpose in this lifetime. It is not for everyone. When an individual makes his way to a contact with one of the Masters, he is not babied and pampered. The Master turns and walks away. He does not look back to see who's following. But those who have to, who must, will. And the time will come when you're ready, he'll meet you there in that special place that only you and he know.

If that is your drum beat, and if this is for you to do, then another day will come, when you will have a special meeting with a Higher Initiate, and you will be ushered into that very select circle known as the Brothers of the Leaf. You will become a Higher Initiate yourself and you will begin a new phase of your journey. It won't be easy. You can't bluff your way through. You will have to work very hard at it. There'll be times you'll wonder if it's worth it. If I've established any credibility with you through all this sharing, then maybe you'll trust me when I say, "It's worth it."

And this leads me to my old promise to give you the secret of how to get through the difficult tests, the increasingly clever tricks of the mind and the ego. Some places that we travel through are very dark. Sometimes we get into dissention, turmoil, doubt, and negativity. The key to a safe passage is deceptively simple. *Always keep your hand in the Master's.* If the time ever comes, and it will, most likely, when what you think and want comes into conflict with what he says, trust him.

If you always like and understand and agree with everything the Master says and does, you will be quite unusual. What he says sometimes isn't nearly as important as what you do with it. The safest way through that is the same thing I said earlier about a detached attitude upon reading the discourses. If it's not your test, it's easy. If you get embroiled in it, with anger, judgments, criticism, analysis, etc., it's your test.

I, long ago, learned not to analyze and chew over such things. I don't always know what he's doing or why, but I always trust that he's the agent of the ECK power and he's doing what has to be done. Sometimes it's for Eckankar, sometimes it's for all of us, sometimes it's just for one of us. But no matter how strange it seems or how hard to understand, he is the ECK and there is a purpose.

When I use this term "Keep your hand in the Master's" it encompasses this understanding and more. As you become more and more familiar with the basic teachings and the spiritual laws, you are aware of the things that are side trips, or traps. You've been warned. If you choose to ignore the warnings and do it anyway, you have to be willing to take full responsibility for your acts—and your hand may be slipping out of the Master's.

The ultimate test is when you are given

a direct, personal order by the Master. Although such situations generally present themselves to a Higher Initiate, that is not always the case. But it's a very special thing, to be given a direct command. And it's beyond my comprehension that anyone, particularly a Higher Initiate, would disobey. But I've seen it happen and I've been struck speechless. Here you are witness to an awesome test. I have such utter respect for it, and its long term ramifications, that I know I once fell there, somewhere in my long, endless journey.

So keeping your hand in the Master's is the secret. It's important all the time, but it's critical when you don't understand what's going on, or when you are faced with a choice that flies in the face of what you know. There will be times when you reach for that hand and you can't find it. You think you've been deserted. Nothing seems right. It's "The Dark Night of Soul." It is then that all you can do is remember your teachings and follow them carefully without having a feel for them. If you do that, it's over soon, and you walk into brighter light than you've ever seen before. And you not only find that hand again, you find yourself encircled in some very powerful, loving arms. As I said before—it's simple. But not always easy.

Stick to the principles and spiritual laws. Know that the Master is the ECK in motion.

There's another thing that works amazingly. I have proved this myself at least a hundred times. Everyone I know has proved it over and again. If you're at the end of your rope in a situation, write the Master a letter and ask for his help. And *know* it's on its way. Often it comes as soon as you mail it. I have set some great records in having the answer before I've even finished writing the letter.

Sometimes, if you're in a Dark Night of Soul, it's hard to write and tell him you're feeling sort of lost and far away and would he help? Let's face it: Who wants to admit that? That's called Pride. And we all know what *that* goes before. You will be stunned at the payoff if you can swallow that pride and bring him your real self who actually does want and need assistance. You are closer to God in such moments. This is very holy ground you stand on here. He knows.

Many ECKists, me included, have had friends or relatives come to us with staggering, seemingly unsolvable problems. The people are not students of Eckankar, they don't have the tool kit we do, and to start them off cold with a bunch of principles and laws is hopeless. But it's odd. If you tell them to write to Harold, that he's very special, and looks after any who come to him, they can usually do that. Many have. And it worked.

My son's girlfriend, Linda, spent a few nights at our house. During her visit she confided to me that a person who didn't like her was practicing witchcraft. Every night for months when she'd fall asleep, this person's face, in huge size, would appear to her and scream at her with angry, threatening words. She was scared to go to sleep. Other things were going wrong in her life. She was a nervous wreck over it. I told her to imagine herself surrounded by a mirror, so that anything the person sent her would reflect back to the sender and not touch her. I do this a lot and it works for me. I went to bed and turned out the light, thinking of her down there trying to do that. Suddenly I knew I'd given her too difficult a task.

I jumped out of bed, went into my office and rummaged through my files until I came up with an old photograph of

Paul. Quietly I opened the door to her room and whispered her name. She was still wide awake.

"Here," I said, "I've got something even better—and you won't have to work." I put the picture of Paul under her pillow. I told her he was a very special being who would protect her. She took the information eagerly.

In the morning, when she came into breakfast, I couldn't wait to hear what had happened in the night. She was wide-eyed in wonder. She told me that sometime in the night she'd felt a cold wind in the room, and then it became black, blacker than any black she'd ever seen. Then suddenly, it was over. Everything was back to normal. She slept peacefully through the night with no invasion of her psyche. A year has gone by. The witch seems to have given up, because Linda has never been bothered since. She has confided, though, that "Paulji" has helped her out of a few other spots, including saving her from an accident on the freeway. She's reading some books. Maybe she'll be reading this one some day.

*I shall tell you a great secret,
my friend. Do not wait for the
last judgment. It takes place
every day.*

—Albert Camus
La Chute 1956

10 <u>Why a Director?</u>

I could write a book on the Masters. So could all my ECKist friends. Maybe that will be the next one that wakes me up in the night.

I've given you some things about how they have worked in my life and in others'. Today I'd like to go into why a Master. Some people don't want one. Since I've been on both sides of that subject, I can understand their reluctance, although knowing what I know now, I find it difficult to envision why anyone would hesitate and pass up so much help. I didn't want it because I was afraid of the commitment. And I mistakenly believed that I would somehow be betraying my old friend, Jesus.

Later I was delighted to make the commitment and understood that my love for Jesus and the way I had made him a very real part of my life, the love I had given to his ideal, had been a necessary step in my personal spiritual evolution. I did not, later, put him down, or throw him away, or turn my back on him. I grew. And I took the growth that training provided me, with me. I was "born again" when I was seventeen. I was born again in 1968 when I met Paul Twitchell. And I have been born again and again ever since. And I do not knock Jesus just because I've grown, anymore than I would have knocked my parents because after they had trained and raised me, I grew and left home. I took with me the training and growth experienced with them. Like everything else I have done in my life, these things are a part of me. They are what made me who I am.

For those who have never had, or have moved beyond, the orthodox experience and are working in the psychic, metaphysical, occult, or higher mind areas, the concept of the Masters and the initiations has been presented at some time or another.

There are people who will spend an entire lifetime, sometimes many, in these areas and have no desire to proceed beyond them. That's fine. In this book I am not talking to anyone who is totally happy and completely satisfied with what they are doing.

I am involved here, with you, the seeker, the adventurer, the curious one, the one who is hungry for what is next. You may have dabbled in any number of the above, but those old feet just had to keep moving. The problem with all those psychic areas I mentioned is that they are lateral. It's another wheel, and one can skip from one spoke to another, always feeling that one is going higher, but for the most part, the motion is circular—and many of the areas of the psychic paths and systems do not resolve *karma* so much as *trade* it.

I cannot tell you how many healers and human helpers I've met who were staggering under the karmic loads they'd taken, quite successfully, from others. Most of them had only meant to do good for their fellow man. But their teachings were not high enough so that they could actually turn it over. Without intending to, *they* took it.

My Brother in Spirit, Tommy, was one. Later, when he made his way to the Master, he realized he'd been a Higher Initiate before in past lives and he'd carried over special knowledge, but incompletely. Before he met Paul Twitchell, he'd healed many people—and he'd taken their illnesses upon himself. Tommy became very prominent in Eckankar, and as he rose in his initiations, he became a fervid and colorful speaker, a familiar sight on the stage. All of us watched the physical ailments of others work themselves through Tommy's body. For several years he went totally blind. He was energetic. Tough. To the point. He didn't believe in babying the chelas. After his Eighth Initiation, my Brother, Tommy, translated to another plane. He had his physical vision back by then, but I guess I'll always remember him, stomping back and forth across the stage, exhorting everyone to listen to him, but not to lean on him, and being blind, marching precariously close to the edge of the stage, where alert assistants were stationed to tell him to be careful. A lot of people were bothered by Tommy because he was a flaming individualist and he was strong, and tough, and outspoken. But he was a real warrior, and he had something valuable for us all.

Even Tommy, and he'd be the first to say it, had to have a Master to guide him through and out of the psychic wheel.

I've already mentioned *The Master Game* by De Ropp. He shows us the necessity for a master to lead us from the trap of chemicals, the idea that spiritual growth in the higher planes can be induced without earning one's passage. Another book of outside reading that graphically showed me the need for the Spiritual Guides is Robert Persig's *Zen and the Art of Motorcycle Maintenance.* In this book we follow the mental trail to the higher states. Persig traveled higher and higher, until he almost had it. Well, he really did have it. The trouble was, he tried to drag his mind through the eye of the needle. Only he didn't know it was his mind and the eye of the needle. His mind hit the light and he went crazy. I believe it took over a hundred shock treatments to settle him back down to a rational, functioning being. Persig lived to tell about it. He came back and wrote a brilliant book about the journey; a brilliant, cautionary tale.

The difference between the student who tries to make his way to the higher worlds without tutelage and guidance is the difference between a man walking a road with many signs and a map in his hand, and a blind man with a cane, turning this way and that, finding trails that only circle back to the main trail, or roads that lead by the longest route imaginable. For this blind man to make it directly to his destination without a guide, it would have to be almost an accident.

Many of us first get the idea we need a Guide when the psychic centers open. That was when the idea first occurred to me. I'd been playing around with ESP and spiritualism, automatic writing, etc. I found out it worked all right. Better than I intended. It got totally out of hand, and I became frightened. I wanted to know more, but sensed I couldn't control the forces I was playing around with. I shut it all off, and thought about the idea of a teacher who could guide me to what I wanted to find without these forces being unleashed in my life. It was another step on the journey; one of those crossroads where the Soul-self prevailed. There was another appointment to keep.

For some people, the difficulty about a Master comes in the area called "Surrender." Obviously, at least I think it's obvious, the act is usually easier for a female than a male. I say, usually, but for any of us, surrender is generally equated with "giving up." The fear is that "Once I do this, this person can own me and my life and I will be helpless." Therefore, we let go in little pieces. We make the Master prove he means us nothing but good will, and that we can trust him completely, and then we surrender a few more pieces. There is nothing wrong with this, that I can see. But then you already know how I went about it. However, my day came and I've never been sorry. I gave over all of it, and it all came back to me, a thousandfold.

I remember the World Wide Seminar in San Francisco. The auditorium was huge and multi-decked. I used to sit in the front rows of these things, but I have changed. Now, in a big auditorium, if you look up in the sparse upper decks you'll see a few loners sitting like birds. If I'm present, that's probably where I'll be.

In San Francisco, Roger, one of my Brothers, and I were perched high up there watching Darwin talk. After he finished, he began to walk down through the crowd, as was his custom. He shook hands with as many as he could. Suddenly Roger jumped up in alarm and said, "Look!" There were people moving in huge masses way off in front who would have converged with him at the last row. We could see Darwin had several Higher Initiates walking with him, but once he reached that converging mass, they would be swallowed up.

As if of one mind, without a word to each other, we began to run. We ran down three flights of stairs, through the long corridor, and into the main hall. To this day I don't know how we did it as fast as we did it. With something approaching superhuman strength we pushed our way through the eager, congealing humanity, who meant Darwin no harm, just wanted to see and maybe touch him, but who could have crushed him with their trapped bodies. I still don't know how we got through them. It's all a blur of excited faces crushing in, and some, really annoyed to be nudged aside, but somehow we managed and found ourselves next to Darwin. Then we turned, and with the other Initiates already with him we physically forced, with our own bodies, openings he could pass through. Later, as we got some space and walked out into the sun, Roger and I walked closely in front of him all the way to the hotel. We didn't say anything, but we both knew that if any harm befell him, it would have to go through us first.

The point is: There was never a thought or a moment's hesitation. I am very small, and the idea that there was danger and that I was not big enough or strong enough, never entered my head. I do not know a Higher Initiate who would not do the same thing, instantly. Those little held-back pieces disappeared long ago. It was as we walked with Darwin in the sun to the hotel that it struck me forcibly: Never, in my entire life, had I cared enough about anything to unhesitatingly risk my life for it. It was a "high" all of its own. I'd come a long, long way from that opinionated jackass who sat in that room so long ago criticizing Paul Twitchell's English.

"I daresay you haven't had much practice,"
said the Queen..."Why, sometimes I've
believed as many as six impossible things
before breakfast!"

—Lewis Carrol
Through the Looking Glass

11 <u>The Magic of It All</u>

When one has been around all this awhile, has gone into the Higher Initiations, and worked through periods of heavy responsibility, especially in direct personal contact with one of the Masters, there is a tendency to become jaded, to begin to take miracles for granted. That's the truth of it, miracles become such an accepted fact, such a normal part of everyday existence for us, that we scarcely take notice of them.

I'm reminded of the lines from a song in *The Flower Drum Song*: "A hundred million miracles are happening every day." They are. And I've been witness to, recipient of, and participant in so many that I could spend the rest of my earthly existence spinning them out for you, and never run out, because all the time I'm spinning my tales new ones are happening.

Webster says a miracle is: "1. An event or action that apparently contradicts known scientific laws. 2. A remarkable event." When one tunes into the Light and the Sound Current, makes the connection with one of the Spiritual Travelers, and begins to work with these factors as a Way of Life, a dimension of experience begins to take place that overrides or extends beyond known scientific laws. I recently heard someone say, "Today's science fiction is tomorrow's science fact." Scientists are loathe to accept anything that cannot be proven under controlled laboratory conditions. This is as it should be for that is their agreed discipline. However, it is not *a priori* that what is not proven is therefore false. Yet, you and I have heard certain self-proclaimed authorities make such statements as, "There is nothing to it. It's never been proven in the lab." I use the term self-proclaimed authorities because such individuals cannot be considered true scientists. Another phenomenon we are witnessing frequently is the researcher with the negative hypothesis. There are quite a few of them these days writing books and appearing on talk shows. A careful hearing reveals some individuals who have designed and structured all research to look only at material that will disprove a theory.

An archeologist working in the ancient

ruins of a canyon in New Mexico was theorizing about the social structure of a past civilization there. His theory as to the foundation of the social system, what explained the location, the structures, the reconstructed society, centered around the access to and control of the flow of water into the canyon. He said that for years he manipulated every discovery in the canyon until it found a comfortable location within his hypothesis. His attention was constantly focused on data that upheld it, while ignoring or giving little attention to data that didn't fit in. To his credit, he later found a new idea, one that demanded he demolish his first construction and follow a whole new concept: That the basis for the social system was not primarily water, but trade. In admitting his error and turning freely to another approach, he furnishes us with an insight we need to keep in mind concerning the process of investigation.

Scientists, since there have been such designations on the planet, have usually fallen into two major categories: Those who cannot or will not budge from a fixed, established concept and those who are open to the new frontiers, the visionaries. The latter create what we call progress and they drag the former along with them, not always without battles and bitterness.

Dr. Elizabeth Kubler-Ross is a prime example of a scientific researcher who pushed the frontier too far for the comfort of the scientific community. The frontier she pushed into is that bridge between this world and the next: the experience called death. She interviewed a number of people who had undergone the experience of being clinically dead, and then through heroic medical efforts were brought back. She asked them if they had any experience they could recall during that period when they were clinically dead. She was totally unprepared for what she heard, but the stories, told by people who were unaware of each other's existence, had a common thread that was impossible to ignore. Dr. Kubler-Ross had no choice. She made that quantum leap, through her own research, into dimensions beyond "proven scientific fact." And even though her scientific credentials are impeccable, she is now undergoing a great deal of criticism and ridicule from certain elements. Her book *On Death and Dying* is a scientific researcher documenting verbatim what Paul Twitchell was describing in his writings ten years before she began her studies.

Science is not ready to concede that there is life after death. But to the subjects of Dr. Kubler-Ross' interviews, it is a proven fact. They experienced leaving their bodies, hovering over the doctors and nurses who were trying to bring them back. Many of them met the being in white light who was standing by. When they were told they had to go back, some of them didn't want to. All of those who recalled the experience had overcome the fear of death.

All of this is to say, that even the things we call miracles today, are not really. They are happenings that operate under another system of laws that the scientists are not yet aware of, but have always existed and many have quietly worked with over the span of civilization.

To any who feel that modern scientific knowledge has reached its zenith, and who look to it as a kind of scripture as to what is and what is not true, one could only wish for more humility. With all this superior technology and computerization they have split the atom and sent man to the moon, but they still don't know how the ancient Egyptians built the pyramids.

Nevertheless, there are many people who are aware of that other set of laws, who know exactly how it was done. The information is available on the planet for those who are determined to find it.

So those folks who are not shut away in boxes explore; they move on into the frontiers, and eventually, the frontier becomes home, and they're off again exploring what is beyond that. And everything in the new frontier seems a miracle to the consciousness of the old one left behind. The explorer looks back on his former miracles and sees only understandable, proven facts.

Of all the illusions I and my colleagues have learned to laugh at, one of the greatest is the notion that divine intervention, miracles, ceased to happen in some ancient biblical era, and somehow we, modern humankind, must be content that the spiritual force no longer overturns earthly laws. What an absolute joke! It's happening all the time. It always was. But not for everyone. Many don't believe it, and they refuse to allow it to take place. They are like the scientist who makes the data fit his hypothesis.

But I believe it. More than that, I KNOW it. And I know hundreds of people who know it. We accept miracles as natural phenomena in our lives. Often they delight us, but they never really surprise us. Why? Because we expect them.

I want nothing less than this for you, my new friend. And if you are in earnest about this journey, if you follow the instructions the Masters have laid down for you, it's yours. But it is not really a gift from me, or even a gift from the Masters. It is a gift you give to yourself.

*I used to go out and walk the beach
quite a bit. And I kept wondering, well,
why me? The selection of me to be the
next Master?...It was a very agonizing
period of my life...this one particular
night when I was walking the beach a very
interesting thing happened. I had come to
the point of where this was almost self-
torture: why should I be the Master?
And I cried out this at one particular
moment, with my clenched fist and looking
up in heaven, saying, "Why? Why me?"
And a voice that seemed to come from all
around me, but I was thinking it was in
back of me, said, "He who is least in
the Kingdom of God shall be the greatest."
And I whirled to see what was going on
or who this was. There was no one there.
There was nothing. But I knew from that
moment on that I had to accept the
responsibility...*

—Paul Twitchell
Excerpt from taped interview with author

12 The Creative Backer: Author of Everything

When people are new to the path they come upon references to Paul as the Mahanta, the Living ECK Master, and they often think these terms mean the same thing. Actually, the Mahanta Consciousness rarely embodies Itself in the physical world. According to a brief memo to himself that I sneaked a peek at on Paul's office wall, there will be only eleven more Mahantas before the end of the world.

There have been thousands of ECK Masters and there may be thousands more before it's over here. But this consciousness will only be embodied on the planet eleven more times. In times of great negativity, of turmoil and unrest, when the spiritual teachings of the era are confused and weakened by corruption and misunderstanding; or they have gone as far as they can go, there is this resurgence of incredible spiritual energy.

The last time this occurred was over

2,000 years ago. People who stand on the piece of the puzzle called "Christianity" say this was because Christ came. But from up above we see much, much more. In a certain time frame, around the Sixth to Fourth Centuries, B.C., there was intense spiritual ferment in the world. In that one period the following people were teaching: Mahavira and Gautama Buddha in India, Zarathustra (Zoroaster) in Persia, Confucius and Lao-Tzu in China, Pythagoras and Socrates in Greece. Among other things the Upanishads and the Bhagavad Gita were written. There is no question of it; the Mahanta Consciousness was personified on the planet at this time. It was everywhere. Some 25 centuries later we are still feeling the effects of it. Christianity actually came quite late in this renaissance, and when one seriously studies what all those great spiritual leaders in 600-400 B.C. were writing and teaching, one finds there was absolutely nothing in the doctrine of Christ that hadn't already been brought up by those earlier teachers, including the sacrifice of a saviour.

The single most important event in

history since those times was the discovery of the atom bomb. The atmospheric testings, according to Paul, ruptured what is known as the Van Allen Belt, which actually serves as a heavy vibratory shield between this world and the psychic plane. A great amount of psychic energy was released upon a planet that was not prepared to cope with it and use it with caution and for constructive purposes. Man, at his stage of evolution, is still a baby and now his newest toys are an atom bomb and a huge bag full of psychic energy. The Mahanta Consciousness appears to balance it out and to set up guidelines and ethics that apply to the energies and problems and consciousness of the era. How long It will be here we don't know. But while It is, there is great turmoil and change. It will take several centuries for an historical overview. Life today is at the center of the vortex, and what is to evolve, what will be set in motion for future generations on the planet is not yet known, except for those gifted individuals who are able to use the ECK-Vidya to view the future. And they say that life is far from over on this planet. In human terms, the end is not near. There is much, much more to come.

Incidentally, as a sidelight to these staggering issues, shortly before he translated from this plane, Paul made a specific request: that the chelas, at all times, pronounce the word Mahanta correctly. It is pronounced *mah hahn' tah*. The word *May hon tay* is used only in chanting. This is a word that is never to be used incorrectly or lightly. One man lost a big commercial contract with Paul because he used the term in a jest. Some people use it as if it's some kind of honorary title that is attached to the title of Living ECK Master. You will notice I use it sparingly for many of the dynamics we've been going over apply to every Living ECK Master, or ECK Masters in general. You don't throw around the term Mahanta casually. It's a very rare and very special thing. When it is said or written, it should be with full awareness of what a unique time we are living in and what a rare thing we are witnessing.

We must have utter respect for what is happening, and although there are bound to be times when we feel overwhelmed by it, there's a way to live with it fairly comfortably. I had to learn this. It was imperative. It would have helped me if I could have learned my own background, what happened in the past that led me to here, but I slammed the door on that possibility in that elevator with Paul. To me, this only means I'm better off not knowing. You live with it comfortably by knowing that whatever it is, you are here for a reason. All is as it should be.

As I said about our daily experiences, sometimes, in the middle of them, we can't really see their true purpose, or where they will lead us. In the historical overview, the same thing applies to the present era in which we are participants. The entire world seems to be engulfed in chaos. The planet is experiencing an infusion of energy. Earthquakes, volcanoes, revolutions, weather changes, etc. are in motion. If we look through a glass darkly, we see political, economic, social, environmental upheaval. But it is not what it seems. When you are able to rise above it all, way above it, what you see is energy. Destruction is not the keynote here; it's *rearrangement*. A new consciousness is in a violent stage of labor. And we have front row seats at the birth taking place. I find it incredibly exciting. But then, I have a tool kit and it enables me to be flexible, to understand that change is not particularly threatening. And my tool kit has enlarged my personal vision so that I am able to see that in spite of our lack of understanding, there is a very precise symmetry and order to all this chaos. It is all a river, and while at times the waters are turbulent and muddy, it never ceases in its inexorable flow to the great sea that is its ultimate destination. You and I are Souls, floating along in the current of this river. Maybe we will get caught up for awhile in an eddy or a side pool, but once again we will enter the mainstream and continue our journey, as will everyone else. Even those you might think of as lost are not really; they're in the stream and eventually will make it.

This is the greatest revelation of all: *Everyone* will make it. It may take more than one lifetime, but there is no way to fail. Hell is not a place, it's a temporary state of consciousness. The whole thing—existence—is a giant balancing scale, and when the *karma* is balanced the journey goes onward to the sea.

This is the most important secret I have to share with you, my friend: What some people call Heaven, some Nirvana, some God-Realization, is inevitable. Sooner or later it is yours—and every other Soul's. There is such a thing as delay, but no such thing as lost. You have been told differently, but it was a lie. Eventually, every Soul comes home. Whether you take a long, slow cruise with many stops or a jet plane, eventually you're going to make it. If you remember nothing else we've shared here, I'll be most content if you remember that.

I've become very fond of these moments we've shared together. It's difficult to disconnect this open line of communication. It's been a wonderful place for me to come to, to turn off the world, and join you in the midst of your journey. But you and I both have work to do, and he's there—waiting. I'll get out of the way and let you two get on with it—and just say, for now, so long. We'll meet again. I'm sure of that. A friend is a friend.

All people stand at different stations in life. One man's stumbling block is another's step to glory. What does it matter when Soul reaches out for the hand of God? It will do so when It is ready.

—Sri Harold Klemp
from an unpublished manuscript

How to Study ECK Further

People want to know the secrets of life and death. In response to this need Sri Harold Klemp, today's spiritual leader of Eckankar, and Paul Twitchell, its modern-day founder, have written special monthly discourses which reveal the Spiritual Exercises of ECK—to lead Soul in a direct way to God.

Those who wish to study Eckankar can receive these special monthly discourses which give clear, simple instructions for the spiritual exercises. The first annual series of discourses is *The ECK Dream Discourses*. Mailed each month, the discourses will offer insight into your dreams and what they mean to you.

The techniques in these discourses, when practiced twenty minutes a day, are likely to prove survival beyond death. Many have used them as a direct route to Self-Realization, where one learns his mission in life. The next stage, God Consciousness, is the joyful state wherein Soul becomes the spiritual traveler, an agent for God. The underlying principle one learns is this: Soul exists because God loves It.

Membership in ECKANKAR includes:

1. Twelve monthly lessons of *The ECK Dream Discourses*, which include these titles: "Dreams—The Bridge to Heaven," "The Dream Master," "How to Interpret Your Dreams," "Dream Travel to Soul Travel," and more. You may study them alone at home or in a class with others.

2. The *Mystic World*, a quarterly newsletter with a Wisdom Note and articles by the Living ECK Master. In it are also letters and articles from students of Eckankar around the world.

3. Special mailings to keep you informed of upcoming Eckankar seminars and activities around the world, new study materials available from Eckankar, and more.

4. The opportunity to attend ECK Satsang classes and book discussions with others in your community.

5. Initiation eligibility.

6. Attendance at certain chela meetings at ECK seminars.

How to Find Out More:

Call **(612) 544-0066,** Monday through Friday, 8 a.m. to 5 p.m. central time, to find out more about how to study *The ECK Dream Discourses*, or use the coupon at the back of this book. Or write: **ECKANKAR, Att: ECK Study, P.O. Box 27300, Minneapolis, MN 55427 U.S.A.**

Introductory Books on ECKANKAR

 The Book of ECK Parables, Volume One,
Harold Klemp

Learn how to find spiritual fulfillment in everyday life from this series of over ninety light, easy-reading stories by Eckankar's spiritual leader, Sri Harold Klemp. The parables reveal secrets of Soul Travel, dreams, karma, health, reincarnation, and—most important of all—initiation into the Sound and Light of God, in everyday settings we can understand.

 ECKANKAR—The Key to Secret Worlds,
Paul Twitchell

Paul Twitchell, modern-day founder of Eckankar, gives you the basics of this ancient teaching. Includes six specific Soul Travel exercises to see the Light and hear the Sound of God, plus case histories of Soul Travel. Learn to recognize yourself as Soul—and journey into the heavens of the Far Country.

 The Wind of Change, Harold Klemp

What are the hidden spiritual reasons behind every event in your life? With stories drawn from his own lifelong training, Eckankar's spiritual leader shows you how to use the power of Spirit to discover those reasons. Follow him from the Wisconsin farm of his youth, to a military base in Japan; from a job in Texas, into the realms beyond, as he shares the secrets of Eckankar.

 The Tiger's Fang, Paul Twitchell

Paul Twitchell's teacher, Rebazar Tarzs, takes him on a journey through vast worlds of Light and Sound, to sit at the feet of the spiritual Masters. Their conversations bring out the secret of how to draw closer to God—and awaken Soul to Its spiritual destiny. Many have used this book, with its vivid descriptions of heavenly worlds and citizens, to begin their own spiritual adventures.

For more information about the books and teachings of Eckankar, please write: **ECKANKAR, Att: Information, P.O. Box 27300, Minneapolis, MN 55427 U.S.A.**

Or look under **ECKANKAR** in your local phone book for an Eckankar Center near you.

There May Be an
ECKANKAR Study Group near You

Eckankar offers a variety of local and international activities for the spiritual seeker. With hundreds of study groups worldwide, Eckankar is near you! Many areas have Eckankar Centers where you can browse through the books in a quiet, unpressured environment, talk with others who share an interest in this ancient teaching, and attend beginning discussion classes on how to gain the attributes of Soul: wisdom, power, love, and freedom.

Around the world, Eckankar study groups offer special one-day or weekend seminars on the basic teachings of Eckankar. Check your phone book under **ECKANKAR**, or call **(612) 544-0066** for membership information and the location of the Eckankar Center or study group nearest you. Or write **ECKANKAR, Att: Information, P.O. Box 27300, Minneapolis, MN 55427 U.S.A.**

☐ Please send me information on the nearest Eckankar discussion or study group in my area.

☐ I would like an application form to study Eckankar further. Please send me more information about the twelve-month Eckankar study discourses on dreams.

Please type or print clearly   941

Name _____

Street _____ Apt. # _____

City _____ State/Prov. _____

Zip/Postal Code _____ Country _____

(Our policy: Your name and address are held in strict confidence. We do not rent or sell our mailing lists. Nor will anyone call on you. Our purpose is only to show people the ECK way home to God.)

ECKANKAR, Att: Information, P.O. Box 27300, Minneapolis, MN 55427, U.S.A.